YOUNG WOMEN OF PRAGUE

Also by Alena Heitlinger

REPRODUCTION, MEDICINE AND THE SOCIALIST STATE
WOMEN AND STATE SOCIALISM
WOMEN'S EQUALITY, DEMOGRAPHY AND PUBLIC POLICIES:
A Comparative Perspective

Also by Susanna Trnka
BODIES OF BREAD AND BUTTER: Reconfiguring Women's Lives in
the Post-Communist Czech Republic (*co-editor with Laura Busheikin*)

Young Women of Prague

Alena Heitlinger

Professor of Sociology
Trent University, Peterborough
Ontario

and

Susanna Trnka

Department of Anthropology
Princeton University
New Jersey

First published 1998 by
MACMILLAN PRESS LTD
Houndmills, Basingstoke, Hampshire RG21 6XS
and London
Companies and representatives
throughout the world

ISBN 0–333–68367–6

A catalogue record for this book is available
from the British Library.

This book is printed on paper suitable for recycling and
made from fully managed and sustained forest sources.

10   9   8   7   6   5   4   3   2   1
07   06   05   04   03   02   01   00   99   98

Printed and bound in Great Britain by
Anthony Rowe Ltd, Chippenham, Wiltshire

For our mothers,
Hana Heitlinger and Nina Trnka,
women of Prague

Contents

Acknowledgements

We should like to thank the Social Sciences and Humanities Research Council of Canada for their generous financial support of this study.

We should also like to acknowledge gratefully the support of friends and colleagues in Prague who discussed the project with us in the initial stages of its formulation. We want to thank in particular Marie Čermáková, Hana Havelková, Karolína Moravcová and Jiřina Šiklová.

Special thanks are due to the principal of one Prague nursing school, who has to remain anonymous in order to ensure privacy to respondents, as well as confidentiality of data. The helpful principal kindly made available to us two class lists of 1989/90 and 1990/1 nursing graduates, from which the sample of women interviewed in this study was drawn. Without the principal's support for this project, and without the willingness of the women to talk and open up their lives to us, this study could not have happened.

1 Introduction

This book is about the lives of young 'ordinary' Czech women who came of age in the aftermath of the November 1989 Velvet Revolution. It is a collection of interviews with fourteen women of similar age and education, but varying work, marital and childbearing experiences. Unlike many informants whose voices 'disappear' in random quotes and aggregate statistics and graphs, our respondents get to speak for themselves, and come across as real personalities. The fourteen chapters of interviews are preceded by a background chapter outlining the social and historical forces that have shaped these women's lives. A concluding chapter analyses common themes emerging out of the interviews, linking them to both legacies of communism and the current postcommunist transition.

DESIGN OF THE STUDY

Conceptual Framework

The main goal of the study, as originally conceived, was to analyse the life strategies towards motherhood and workforce participation of a cohort of Czech women who came of age in the aftermath of the November 1989 Velvet Revolution. The notion of a 'life strategy' contains three key elements: individual exercise of choice (typically involving careful cost–benefit evaluation of several alternatives); a set of options from which to choose; and an extended time-frame (Palomba and Sabbadini, 1993). Having an individual plan of action, and being prepared to carry it out, implies an attempt to control future outcomes in the presence of risk and uncertainty (Ní Bhrolcháin, 1993).

It goes without saying that available life strategies and opportunities differ according to prevailing social norms, economic and political conditions, the size and composition of successive birth cohorts, one's gender, age, ethnicity, health, personal contingencies, and situational incentives. Belonging to a specific birth cohort brings about a unique set of life choices and opportunities. As each

1

cohort ages, it confronts a different set of historical forces, which may entail relative advantages or disadvantages in life chances.

Birth cohorts are most sharply differentiated during periods of accelerated change. However, the potential for change is not distributed equally across cohorts. It is most pronounced for cohorts of young adults who are old enough to participate in societal transformations, but not old enough to have become committed to existing social arrangements. A cohort of young adults provides both a market for new ideas and a source of new followers, thus facilitating the development of new orientations towards major social institutions. Traumatic episodes (such as war or a revolution) may become the foci of crystallization of a distinct mentality of a cohort (Mannheim, 1952; Ryder, 1965; Riley *et al.*, 1972; Elder, 1978; Gerson, 1985).

The experiences of the first adult cohorts confronting new emerging norms and practices are usually quite special. Having few role models to imitate and lacking in socialization to norms and values that are consonant with the demands of a new era, individuals comprising those cohorts have to accommodate to their new social options through trial and error. Subsequent cohorts' historical experiences and life strategies are likely to be quite different, as the once radical ideas and practices become routinized and institutionalized (Foner, 1978). Birth cohorts and their aging thus offer an important framework in which to study change and continuity in life-course patterns and social norms.

Because of structured variations in exposure to, and interpretation of, societal conditions (by class, gender, region and ethnicity), it is essential that analysis of whole cohorts be complemented by analysis of life-course variation *within* cohorts (Elder, 1978).

Methodology

Statistics on changes and continuities in marriage, divorce, remarriage, time spent on domestic work, contraceptive use, abortion, fertility, secondary and postsecondary education, workforce participation and so on, cannot provide any information on variation in meaning which life-course events have for individuals. Nor can they help with testing empirically the validity of describing behaviour as strategic. To give women their own voices, and to account for diversity of experiences *within* specific birth cohorts, this study is based on testimonies collected through interviews with a carefully selected group of women. As in all qualitative research, sampling was based

upon analytical criteria rather than on random statistical repre-
sentativeness (Riley, 1963; Huberman and Miles, 1994).

Our sample of women belongs to the first cohort of young adults
to confront and embody emerging postcommunist norms and practices. It was drawn from two class lists of 1989/90 and 1990/1 nursing graduates. These lists were kindly made available to us by the
principal of one Prague nursing high school (out of ten such schools
in the city). Selecting two anonymous classes of approximately 30
students each out of 120 graduates in an unnamed school has en-
sured privacy to our respondents, as well as confidentiality of data.
All names used in this book are pseudonyms. All of the interviews
have been edited and in some of the interviews any personal characteristics which could identify the respondent have been altered.

As is evident from our study, Czech nursing graduates offer a
fairly representative mix of class backgrounds, personal relations,
career aspirations, work achievements (which are by no means limited
to nursing), and resolutions of conflicts between work, marriage
and motherhood.[1] Under communism, a nursing qualification required only a specialized high school education of four years duration. This meant that most aspiring nurses entered training at the
very young age of 14–15, and graduated by the age of 18–19, or at
the most 20. At the time of the interviews, the respondents were
23–25 years old, i.e. at an age when conflicts between forging a
work identity and creating a family are especially acute. The 23
interviews, of which 14 are included in this book, were conducted
in Czech by Susanna Trnka during the period of November 1995–
February 1996. The main objective of the interviews was to learn
what young Czech women have to say about their lives and the
postcommunist transition to a market economy and a democracy.

The original research design envisaged completely open-ended,
unstructured, conversational interviews, in order to avoid framing
questions in such a way that they would impose inappropriate ex-
ternal meanings and interpretations of experience. We thought,
somewhat naively, that after explaining the purpose of the study,
we would simply let the respondents tell us 'their own stories'. We
were also committed to broadly conceived feminist 'standpoint
methodologies' that are concerned with portraying women's experiences from the point of view of those who live them. We wanted
to rely on feminist interviewing techniques that emphasize trust,
empathy, careful listening, and active involvement of respondents
in the construction of data about their lives (Finch, 1984; Fontana

and Frey, 1994; Oakley, 1981; Olesen, 1994; Reinhartz, 1992; Smith, 1987, 1992; Stanley and Wise, 1990).

However, as is often the case with research projects, things did not work out quite as planned. First of all, the concept of 'life-strategies' turned out to have had limited applicability to the pre-1989 communist period. As we noted, life strategies are about individual attempts to control future outcomes in the presence of risk and uncertainty. However, during the communist era – characterized, among other things, by full employment and a comprehensive system of direct and indirect social welfare measures and pronatalist fiscal incentives awarded to families and mothers – the majority of Czech people led fairly homogenous, stable and predictable lives, with little need for life-strategies. The main life-course events under communism were fairly predictable: secondary education, apprenticeship or post-secondary education, followed by life-long gainful employment combined with marriage and motherhood at an early age (late teens or early 20s). The notion of a life-strategy is obviously more relevant in the postcommunist context, in which the Czech Republic is gradually becoming a market-oriented liberal democracy of the Western type.

While retaining our commitment to feminist standpoint methodologies and interviewing techniques, we found it necessary to use semi-structured rather than completely open-ended interviews. In order to impose some unity on the interviews, all respondents were asked a broadly similar set of questions, though not necessarily in the same order.

CONDUCTING THE INTERVIEWS

Almost all of the informants were initially contacted by telephone. The few who did not have a telephone received letters. In either case, they were given a brief description of the project, told that their name was obtained from their previous school principal, and, when possible, informed of how many members of their class had already been interviewed. Those who expressed interest were offered the choice of meeting in their homes, or in a public area, usually at a cafe or restaurant, either in the centre of the city or in their own neighbourhoods. Even though most of the participants lived in the same neighbourhood as their former nursing school, which was about 20 minutes tram journey from the city centre, the majority chose to meet in cafes in the city centre, many of them stating that they welcomed the chance to go downtown.

In order to be able to find each other in a public setting, it was necessary for the participants and the interviewer to exchange descriptions of themselves. Usually, they mentioned what they would be wearing. But sometimes participants' descriptions of themselves were more creative. For example, one woman described herself as 'a petite brunette who is very obviously pregnant'. The interviewer usually described herself by telling the participants that she was about the same age as them, and that she would be carrying a small tape recorder. All of the interviews were taped. They were carried out in Czech, without the aid of an interpreter.

Those participants who chose to be interviewed in their own homes were usually mothers of infants. With one exception, they lived in *paneláks* – large, concrete, prefabricated housing blocks that sprawl for miles at the edge of the city. Interviews usually took place over a cup of coffee or tea in the women's living room or kitchen.

Every effort was made to make the interviews as relaxed as possible. The participant and the interviewer usually chatted before the formal interview started about the project. Women were encouraged to ask any questions they might have, but usually they held onto their questions until after the official interview was concluded.

While most of the women showed interest in the questions and answered with genuine thoughtfulness, for the most part they did not introduce other issues, go off on tangents, or attempt to steer the interview in other directions. However, after the tape recorder was turned off, many of them returned to elaborate upon certain topics. For example, one woman (whose interview is not included in this collection) answered all of the questions in two or three brief sentences. When asked about her religion, she simply shrugged. But once the 'official' questions were over, she launched into detailed explanation of her views of death and reincarnation that lasted approximately two hours. While she might be an extreme example, in general participants seemed to clearly distinguish between 'formal responses' to interview questions and the informal discussion afterwards.

While the formal interview questions usually took about an hour to an hour and a half to discuss, the interviews themselves lasted anywhere from an hour to three and a half hours. As with any other meeting between strangers, sometimes the participant and the interviewer were able to find common interests and develop a sense of 'rapport' on certain issues, and sometimes they fell short of this. In few cases, the participant and interviewer agreed to meet a second time to continue discussing topics such as feminism, education, and health care in the US, on a more informal basis. With the exception of Jana, who was formally interviewed twice, further discussions between the interviewer and the participant were understood to be informal and confidential, and not specifically drawn upon in our study.

By far, the majority of questions that participants asked the interviewer were either personal ones about the interviewer herself, or more general questions about life in the US. Very few people asked anything about the project itself, except to express curiosity about the lives of their classmates.

The most popular question asked about the United States was: 'Is life in the US really like *Beverly Hills 90210* or *Bay Watch*?' This question was usually asked with a tone of skepticism: 'Americans really can't be as silly as the characters on 90210?' one woman queried. Another popular, but dated, comparison was to the television serial Dallas. This programme was not shown on Czechoslovak TV during the communist period, and was therefore broadcast on Czech TV for the first time almost two decades after its heyday in the United States. Other common questions were about housing and education in the US. Participants often asked whether Americans have as much trouble finding apartments as they themselves do. As the Czech Republic is slowly moving towards charging students tuition for their education, many of them were curious about how this system works in the US. They were also interested in the problems Western women encounter in their efforts to juggle family and a job. Many expressed shock when they found out about American maternity leave policies, whose provisions are the worst in the developed world.[2] Very few of the respondents asked any questions about health care in the United States.

Women usually steered clear of political or other contentious issues. There were, however, two exceptions. Magda took the interview as an opportunity to air her strong anti-American sentiments. Alexandra, in addition to criticizing the current Czech president, Václav Havel, espoused a heated rhetorical defence of capital punishment.

After being asked so many personal questions themselves, most of the participants seemed to enjoy turning the tables. Often the first thing the interviewer was asked was, 'Why aren't you married?' or 'When do you plan to have children?' One participant simply asked: 'And how would you have answered the same questions?' A few times, the questions took on a more confrontational tone. For example, one participant disapprovingly demanded to know why the interviewer wasn't wearing makeup and why her hair was pulled back in a pony tail.

It is interesting to note that while the interviewer made an attempt to dress casually and to relate to the participants in an informal way, the participants tended to comment that they had expected someone 'different'. 'Older' they usually explained. 'More severe' was one comment. Many participants expressed curiosity about the interviewer's background: 'How did you learn to speak Czech?' and 'Why as an American do you have a Czech name?' were common questions. But once they found out that her parents are Czech immigrants who left Czechoslovakia in 1968, most of them left this potentially contentious political topic alone.

The most difficult stumbling block the interviewer encountered was with participants who agreed to be interviewed but never showed up for their appointments. This happened in about 30–40 per cent of the scheduled interviews. Even though the interviewer had given the participants her home number, no one called in advance to cancel. Some people even employed clever tactics to avoid being recontacted by phone. For example, one woman agreed to an interview, but said that she had to check her schedule, and that the interviewer should phone her later that afternoon. When the interviewer called her back, she reached the woman's grandmother, who said the woman was out. 'I'll just try her later then', the interviewer said. 'No, she won't be back today', her grandmother replied. 'Then can I try tomorrow?', the interviewer asked. 'No, she won't be here then.' It was obvious that the woman would never be at home.

A more extreme case was a woman who agreed to an interview, but requested that it would take place in the interviewer's home (this was the only such request). 'She and her husband would drive over and leave the baby with her mother', she explained. When she did not show up, the interviewer called her home and was told by her mother that the woman must surely be there already, since she had left the house over an hour ago. Another hour passed and then the woman herself called the interviewer to angrily complain that she had come to the building where the interviewer lived and searched in vain for the interviewer's name among the directory of names at the front door. (In the majority of Czech apartment buildings the front door is locked and there is a directory of names and bells to ring for entry.) She assured the interviewer that she had the right address but that 'the door was locked, and your name wasn't on any of the bells, so I couldn't get in'. What this woman did not know was that the interviewer lived in one of the few buildings in Prague without a directory and without door bells at the front door. In fact, the front door was always left unlocked during the day.

The above examples are described in detail not to explain why there was a such a low response rate, but because the women's ways of avoiding being interviewed are interesting in their own right. A number of other researchers and journalists working in Prague told us that they encountered similar problems with 'no-shows', and that our no-show rate was actually quite good. In our case, there developed a clear pattern of recurring initial acceptance on the part of the participant. Out of the many women who did not want to be interviewed, only two actually said 'no'. All of the others initially agreed, and then contrived complicated ways of getting out of their acceptance.

When the interviewer actually asked participants themselves (those who were interviewed) why so many of their classmates were not showing up, they expressed no surprise, and explained it as the Czechs' 'inability to say no'. 'You must understand that Czechs still don't know how to say no', one participant explained, 'It's much easier just to say yes and then not show up.'

One participant, Olina, also suggested that perhaps they were afraid of meeting a stranger. She herself had feared that the interviewer might be a deranged maniac who would 'drag her into the bushes', she explained. So after the interview was set up, but before she decided whether or not to go, she had phoned her school principal to check on the interviewers' references. A second participant also stated that she had called the school to make sure the interviewer really was who she said she was.

Given this amount of apprehension and sometimes downright fear, it is clear why it was sometimes difficult to create a relaxed, informal atmosphere. It is also clearer now why the participants did not feel comfortable taking the interviews in various directions, offering their life histories, or generally taking charge in shaping the interview experience to express their particular perspectives.

That said, women did shape the interview experience in various ways. They expressed great interest in some subjects, and boredom with respect to others. They also introduced themes that the interviewer had not raised. In the following pages there is a wealth of information, both on topics we had thought about as well as issues that the women introduced to us as being important.

In general, our questions covered issues of gender roles within their families of origin, as well as within their own families; their perceptions of motherhood/fatherhood and family life; their thoughts on their education and on nursing in general; their job experiences and thoughts on work; their opinions on the health care system; their plans as teenagers, and their current plans for the future; and how they saw the political and economic changes following the 1989 revolution effecting their lives. In addition, women spoke at great length about other issues that interested them, such as: housing problems; the importance of travel and learning a foreign language; the importance of their grandmothers in their lives; their thoughts on beauty; the role of violence in their lives; sexuality and the availability of contraception; the importance of money; and their perception of Western Europe and the US. (All of these topics are discussed in greater detail in the final chapter of this book.)

Our thanks go out to each woman we interviewed for her time, her patience and co-operation, and her willingness to open up her life not only to us, but to the readers of this book.

NOTES

1. What our small sample could not capture is diversity by ethnicity and sexual orientation. There were no women in our study who defined themselves as Jewish, Gypsy, lesbian or bisexual.
2. Measures associated with the 'social protection of motherhood' were key areas of privilege women in the communist countries enjoyed over those in capitalist ones. By the late 1970s, the Czechoslovak government was spending almost 4 per cent of its annual budget on direct cash benefits for the family and an additional 7 per cent on services and subsidies in kind. These levels exceed comparable expenditures of any other major developed country. Czech women have become quite accustomed to a range of family-oriented services and allowances provided by the state, including generous maternity leave provisions. By the end of the communist period, all childbearing women in Czecho-

slovakia were guaranteed 26 weeks of paid maternity leave (35 weeks for single mothers and mothers with multiple births). From 1970, mothers could also take advantage of the so-called maternity (or childcare) allowance, paying mothers a flat rate (amounting to substantially less than their average monthly income) to stay at home with their child until it reached three years of age. As a pronatalist measure designed to encourage fertility, eligibility for the allowances started only with the birth of the second or subsequent child (Heitlinger, 1987, pp. 64–71). Fearing a sharp increase in unemployment, the first postcommunist government has *improved* these provisions. The 1990 law governing maternity allowances extended payments to previously excluded women (such as mothers with only one child or women who have never been employed), and for the first time made them available to fathers as well. The job-protected leave was subsequently extended for another year to four years (Heitlinger, 1993a). The young women in our study were quite shocked to learn that, prior to 1993, women in the US could obtain job-protected leave and some income support immediately before and immediately after childbirth only as a fringe benefit negotiated individually or as part of collective bargaining between employees and employers. Under the first Clinton administration, unpaid family leave of 12 weeks became a statutory right. However, the mandatory legislation only covers companies with 50 or more employees. The United States is the only developed country without a general right to a maternity leave (Heitlinger, 1993b, pp. 190–1).

REFERENCES

Elder, Glen H., Jr (1978), 'Approaches to Social Change and the Family', in John Demos and Sarane Spence Boocock (eds), *Turning Points: Historical and Sociological Essays on the Family* (Chicago, IL: University of Chicago Press).
Finch, Janet (1984), '"It's Great to Have Someone to Talk to": The Ethics and Politics of Interviewing Women', in Helen Roberts (ed.), *Social Researching: Politics, Problems, Practice* (London: Routledge & Kegan Paul).
Foner, Anne (1978), 'Age Stratification and the Changing Family', in John Demos and Sarane Spence Boocock (eds), *Turning Points: Historical and Sociological Essays on the Family* (Chicago, IL: University of Chicago Press).
Fontana, Andrea and Frey, James H. (1994), 'Interviewing: The Art of Science', in Norman K. Denzin and Yvonna S. Lincoln (eds), *Handbook of Qualitative Research* (Thousand Oaks, CA: Sage).
Gerson, Kathleen (1985), *Hard Choices: How Women Decide about Work, Career, and Motherhood* (Berkeley, CA: University of California Press).
Heitlinger, Alena (1987), *Reproduction, Medicine and the Socialist State* (London: Macmillan; New York: St Martin's Press).

Heitlinger, Alena (1993a), 'The Impact of the Transition from Communism on the Status of Women in the Czech and Slovak Republics', in Nanette Funk and Magda Mueller (eds), *Gender Politics and Post-Communism: Reflections from Eastern Europe and the Former Soviet Union* (New York and London: Routledge), pp. 95–108.

Heitlinger, Alena (1993b), *Women's Equality, Demography and Public Policies: A Comparative Perspective* (London: Macmillan Press/New York: St Martin's Press).

Huberman, Michael A. and Miles, Matthew B. (1994), 'Data Management and Analysis Methods', in Norman K. Denzin and Yvonna S. Lincoln (eds), *Handbook of Qualitative Research* (Thousand Oaks, CA: Sage).

Mannheim, Karl (1952), 'The Problem of Generations', in *Essays on the Sociology of Knowledge* (Oxford and New York: Oxford University Press), Chapter 7.

Ní Bhrolcháin, Máire (1993), 'Women's and Men's Life Strategies in Developed Societies', in International Union for the Scientific Study of Population, *International Population Conference, Montreal 1993, 24 August–1 September*, Vol. 2 (Liege: IUSSP).

Oakley, Ann (1981), 'Interviewing Women. A Contradiction in Terms', in Helen Roberts (ed.), *Doing Feminist Research* (London: Routledge & Kegan Paul).

Olesen, Virginia (1994), 'Feminism and Models of Qualitative Research', in Norman K. Denzin and Yvonna S. Lincoln (eds), *Handbook of Qualitative Research* (Thousand Oaks, CA: Sage).

Palomba, Rossella and Sabbadini, Linda Laura (1993), 'Female Life Strategies: The Way of Compromise', in International Union for the Scientific Study of Population, *International Population Conference, Montreal 1993, 24 August–1 September*, Vol. 2 (Liege: IUSSP).

Reinharz, Shulamit (1992), *Feminist Methods in Social Research* (New York and Oxford: Oxford University Press).

Riley, Matilda White (1963), *Sociological Research*, vol. 1: *A Case Approach* (New York: Harcourt, Brace & World).

Riley, Matilda White, Jonson, Marilyn and Foner, Anne (1972), *Aging and Society: A Sociology of Age Stratification*, vol. 3 (New York: Russell Sage).

Ryder, Norman B. (1965), 'The Cohort as a Concept in the Study of Social Change', *American Sociological Review*, **30** (December).

Smith, Dorothy E. (1987), *The Everyday World as Problematic* (Boston, MA: Northeastern University Press).

Smith, Dorothy E. (1992), 'Sociology from Women's Experience: A Reaffirmation', *Sociological Theory*, **10**.

Stanley, Liz and Wise, Sue (1990), 'Method, Methodology and Epistemology in Feminist Research Process', in Liz Stanley (ed.), *Feminist Praxis, Research, Theory and Epistemology in Feminist Sociology* (London and New York: Routledge).

2 The Broader Context

The women interviewed in this book were born and went to school during the communist period, but their adult work and family identities were forged under the very different circumstances of the post-communist transition to a market economy and a democracy. They represent the first group of young adults who are old enough to participate in societal transformations, but not old enough to have become committed to previous social arrangements. As in any revolutionary transition, there have been both continuities and discontinuities with the past, since historical legacies have influenced the course of the transition to capitalism.

In order to situate and contextualize the lives of the nursing graduates interviewed for this book, this chapter examines some important aspects of Czech history and culture, the main characteristics of communism, the post-communist transition, several nursing issues (such as education, pay and working conditions), and the dominant gender ideologies of 'women's nature' and 'women's place'.

THE HISTORICAL, CULTURAL AND POLITICAL LEGACIES

Although the Czechs date their national history to the Great Moravian state in the ninth century, the modern Czech national identity was formed only in the nineteenth century, during the process of national 'awakening'. The Czechs lost their independence in 1620, when Czech Protestant nobles were defeated by Austria in the Battle of White Mountain, the first battle of the Thirty Years War. The next two and a half centuries of Czech history, generally referred to as the 'Period of Darkness', were marked by re-Catholicization and Germanization. The Habsburgs' efforts led to the virtual disappearance of the Czech language in the urban areas, and to a widespread deep suspicion against the Catholic Church. As the Czech journalist Daniel Kumermann (1996, p. 12) put it, since the mid-seventeenth century, 'a rather primitive, but quite fervent, generalization has been made that Catholicism comes from a foreign, occupying power and it pits itself against locally bred Czech Protestantism. This dichotomy is one of the main reasons why the modern Czech Republic is one of the most secular nations in the world.' Opinion polls estimate that four out of five Czechs consider themselves either atheist or agnostic (Legge, 1996).

The founders of the modern Czech national movement made the religious reformer Jan Hus (who in 1415 was burnt at the stake as a heretic) and his followers the centrepiece of Czech history. Czech nationalists focused their efforts initially on the rehabilitation of the Czech language – but, as the movement expanded, the predominantly cultural definition of the Czech national identity gradually gave way to a more political conception, and to demands for political sovereignty.

Czechoslovakia, a common state of Czechs and their neighbours, the Slovaks, arose in 1918 as one of several successor states to the Austro-Hungarian Empire. The First Czechoslovak Republic (1918–39) was a rich and economically advanced country, as the Czech lands inherited two-thirds of the industrial base of the Austro-Hungarian Empire. Slovakia, in contrast to the Czech lands, was an economically undeveloped area, with a strong Catholic influence and a distinct language. However, the two languages, Czech and Slovak, are mutually understandable without much difficulty.

Czechoslovakia in the inter-war period was a democratic, multicultural and ethnically diverse state, the only Western-type liberal democracy in the whole of Eastern and Central Europe. The Germans constituted the largest ethnic minority – some 3 million people out of a population of 15 million. Ethnic tensions between the Czechs and the Germans, and between the Czechs and the Slovaks, marked the whole period of the First Republic, which lasted until its break-up in March 1939.

The September 1938 Munich agreement, which was sanctioned by Czechoslovakia's allies, Britain and France, forced Czechoslovakia to cede to Hitler's Germany the predominantly German-speaking Sudeten lands. The subsequent occupation of the now-truncated Bohemia and Moravia by Nazi Germany in March 1939, and the simultaneous creation of a separate clerical–fascist Slovak state, provided powerful legitimation to strong anti-German (and anti-Slovak) sentiments. As the Czech researcher Kateřina Pekárková (1995, p. 69) put it, 'the occupation of the Czech part of Czechoslovakia by Germany during the Second World War was, for the Czech population, nothing more than the confirmation of the 19th century image of Germans as an aggressive and hostile nation'.

Memories of the German occupation continue to shape contemporary Czech anti-German sentiments in the Czech Republic (reflected in the interviews with Monika and Petra), as do fears that the Sudeten Germans (and their descendants) expelled after the end of the Second World War will want to reclaim confiscated property. The majority of the Czech population does not consider the postwar expulsion of the Sudeten Germans as a criminal act of 'ethnic cleansing'. Instead, the expulsion is generally regarded as an act of justice for treason against the Czechoslovak state, and as a just retribution for the overwhelming support the Sudeten Germans gave to Hitler.

The Nazi genocide against the Jews and the Gypsies, the postwar expulsion of the Sudeten Germans, the ceding of the Carpathian Ukraine to the Soviet Union, and the installation of the communist regime in 1948, transformed the ethnic composition and the cultural and political milieu of the country. As Pekárková (1995, p. 69) argues, 'the former multicultural and ethnically mixed society, whose heterogeneity had created a unique intellectual environment, especially in centres like Prague, was destroyed'. Pekárková considers the processes of ethnic cleansing 'without feeling guilt', and of creating a 'parochial monoculture', as important factors underlying the ambiguous, if not overtly hostile, attitudes towards cultural diversity that one finds in the Czech Republic today.

THE COMMUNIST PERIOD, 1948–89

Work, Family and Politics

Czechoslovak communism was based on the dominant features of the Soviet model. It included a politically dominant communist party; restrictions on freedom of expression and foreign travel; a state-owned, centrally controlled and planned economy; and an industrialization strategy based on an expanding labour force rather than on improving productivity. It was also characterized by wage disparities between the 'preferred' industrial occupations, largely dominated by men, and the 'non-preferred' occupations in the basically feminized service sector, as well as by a severely undeveloped consumer sector. Furthermore, there was an official commitment to women's equality based on the Marxist–Leninist approach to women's emancipation.

Nearly everything about the public spheres of education, worklife and politics was officially prescribed. The party-state had full control over the economy and the interpretation of official ideology. Thus, individual participation in public organizations was motivated more by the desire to curry favour with the communist regime and less by aspirations to accomplish concrete things. A genuine sense of being politically active could not be achieved under communism, as all aspects of public life were directed by the communist party-state.

In contrast to Western-style market economies, the economies of the former communist societies in East Central Europe were consumer-weak. Low priority was given to easing women's household responsibilities through domestic labour-saving devices such as dishwashers, convenience shopping, etc. There was no concept of consumer service and satisfaction. In order to obtain goods and services in short supply, or to improve their quality, consumers were frequently forced to resort to bribes. For the client, there was little difference between a physician, a car dealer, or a plumber in this respect, although bribing a physician for a medically necessary treatment or life-saving drugs in short supply might literally be a matter of life and death, and as such be considered a high priority. Offering and accepting 'under-the-counter' payments was part of what the Hungarian émigré economist István Kemény (1982) called the shadow market, where providers of a service (e.g. physicians and nurses) used gratuities to adjust low salaries imposed on them by central authorities. However, by accepting bribes, physicians and nurses undermined one of the key claims to a professional status – the rendering of an altruistic service to the public.

Education, merit and work performance were severely devalued. Statistics reveal that in the 1980s only 10 per cent of young women achieved university education. A higher proportion – 40 per cent – graduated from apprenticeship programmes, and another 40 per cent were high/vocational school graduates. The remaining 10 per cent entered employment at the age of 14–15 upon the completion of compulsory elementary schooling. The figures for males were broadly similar; 50 per cent graduated from apprenticeship programmes; 26 per cent obtained secondary education; 14 per cent had a university qualification; and 10 per cent left school at the age of fifteen (Kučera and Fialová, 1996, p. 15).

The Czech sociologist Petr Matějů (1992) found in his 1989 survey of life strategies that neither adults nor children considered education or skills as crucial to life success. Instead, economic and political success was linked to family self-sufficiency and to participation in the parallel shadow market economy. Since nearly everything about worklife was prescribed by the party-state, work activities in the public sphere were often considered less important for one's identity, prestige and income than private family-based activities. The latter (including male-dominated 'moonlighting' in the parallel second economy) were relatively free from party-state control and, as such, more highly regarded. Women played a major role in the socially dominant family sphere because of their roles as homeworkers and mothers.

As the Czech social philosopher Hana Havelková (1993a, p. 92) argues,

> because public work was a means to political blackmail and productivity was not the main criterion for remuneration, work in the public sphere and professional careers in particular lost their prestige. The result was a specific and unnatural separation of the value of work itself and the value of a career. The criterion of personal prestige gradually became tied to one's family image. The family turned into the dominant social institution, to the extent that we can almost consider it a public institution. There was also a countereffect to this tendency. While the family remained the last bastion of freedom, the workplace remained the last gathering place outside the family. Both private and public problems were discussed at work, and often work time was partially devoted to arranging private matters.

Nursing and the Health Care System

Like its Soviet counterpart, the Czechoslovak socialist health care system was a state-operated, tax-financed, specialized branch of the general public service. The communist party-state exercised tight budgetary control over health care facilities, technologies, drugs and salaries, and a high degree of administrative power over health norms and standards. With few exceptions (e.g. the special clinics for the party *nomenklatura*, the army and railway workers), the entire health service was centralized under the Czech and Slovak ministries of health.[1] The communist authorities assigned low priority to health care (along with other social services), regarding it as a 'nonproductive' sector of the economy secondary to industrial development. It was funded accordingly, and wages in the 'non-productive' sectors were much lower than in the productive industrial sectors.

Czechoslovak nursing during the communist period did not fit any of the defining characteristics of a profession or a 'semi-profession'. There was no prolonged period of training, no abstract body of knowledge, and no self-governance. Czech nurses had virtually no professional status, autonomy or prestige, and their official incomes were well below the average industrial wage (Heitlinger, 1995).

Nurses belonged to the category of 'middle-level' health care workers, a category which also included physiotherapists, opticians, X-ray technicians, and pharmaceutical and dental laboratory technicians. The term 'middle-level' reflected an occupational requirement for a 'middle-level' vocational education, which was acquired at specialized four-year nursing high schools.[2] What this meant was that the majority of aspiring nurses entered training at the very young age of 14–15 when they lacked the social maturity as well as the self-confidence and responsibility one typically associates with adults. As indicated in several of the interviews, our respondents did not think that entering nursing training at the age of fourteen was a good thing, although several admitted that the nursing high school had helped them to achieve adult maturity.

The recruitment and training for nursing, nurses' relations with patients and allied health practitioners, and the quality of service provided, were also shaped by the specifics of gender. Virtually all Czechoslovak nurses were women, and their career aspirations were not very high. Low educational requirements meant that nurses did not invest much in their training, and this in turn made the cost of leaving the occupation quite low. Twenty per cent of nurses left nursing annually, for most part only a few years after entering practice. Most nurses who left were in their early twenties (Mellanová, 1993).

The Specifics of Gender under Communism

Like other communist regimes in East Central Europe, Czechoslovakia adopted a Marxist–Leninist approach to women's equality. It was based on Engels' hypothesis that the emancipation of women would result from the abolition of private property, the productive employment of women and the socialization of private domestic work and childcare. Stalinist writings in particular equated women's emancipation with a high level of female labour force participation in a socialist economy (Scott, 1974; Heitlinger, 1979; Wolchick, 1979, 1981a, b). The dominant image during the early communist period was that of a heroic worker 'who speaks at meetings and struggles against the imperialists' (Hauser, n.d., p. 2).

The communist industrialization strategy had contradictory implications for women's equality. The pattern of economic growth, based on a quantitative expansion of the labour force, dictated a substantial increase both in the full-time employment of women and in the social provision for maternity and childcare. The communist party- state guaranteed employment (though not equal pay), and was effectively the sole provider of social welfare. In turn, welfare provision gave the party-state its most potent and pervasive instrument of social and political control, and its principal guarantee of political stability and legitimacy. The 'social protection of motherhood' was generally welcomed and taken for granted by women, who became quite accustomed to a range of family-oriented services and allowances provided by the paternalistic welfare state.

Thus, several of the demands of Western feminist movements during the 1970s, for equal educational and employment opportunities, childcare facilities, access to abortion and extended maternity leaves, were already implemented, and taken for granted, in state socialist Czechoslovakia. However, the value of the family-oriented cash and tax benefits was low relative to the average wage and actual cost of raising children (Heitlinger, 1987, pp. 256–61). Moreover, the quality of state childcare facilities was quite poor. Low standards were manifested in such things as high rates of sickness among children, high child-to-care-giver ratios, and impersonal or over-regimented attitudes towards children by the predominantly female staff. Many parents were reluctant to place their children in state day care facilities, and the decline in the number of these institutions has generated little public controversy (Heitlinger, 1993).

While paying lip service to equality, the communist leadership not only never challenged gender stereotyping, but actually encouraged the preservation of conventional sex roles. Many expert advice books urged women to accept the existing gender hierarchy, and to preserve marital harmony by not 'nagging' men to help them with housework. The pronatalist policies adopted in the early 1970s also reinforced the idea that childrearing and domestic work are 'by nature' women's work (Scott, 1974; Heitlinger, 1979, 1987, 1993; Wolchik 1979, 1981a).

Throughout the Czechoslovak communist period, the role of women was defined as a harmony between economic, maternal and political functions. There was no such parallel father–worker role for men. The dominant model for women was that of wife–mother occupied in a job, rather than in a professional career (Heitlinger, 1979, 1987). Although married women did not have the duty to be employed, practically all of them were. Male wages were never high enough to enable men to become the sole supporters of their families. An additional reason why mothers did not give up their jobs was that, in principle, they found both roles to be manageable. Many women were employed in lower-paid jobs that did not require very demanding work, and that situation allowed them to combine domestic and waged work. Clerical jobs were especially popular, because they enabled women to do their shopping and arrange for many other family needs during working hours (Havelková, 1993b).

Women took deliberate refuge in motherhood and the 'double burden' to escape political manipulation and to give a more positive meaning to their lives. Political blackmail usually took the form of linking professional advancement with joining the Communist Party. In contrast to the politically tainted public sphere of work and politics, the individual family was a 'free sphere' where people could be their 'authentic' selves and resist the intrusion of the all-pervasive communist party-state.[3] As a women's domain, the family thus provided women with a certain amount of power, authority and creativity. Women therefore opted for a 'cult of motherhood', and children provided an 'excuse' for not joining the Communist Party. Even though the 'double burden' resulted in a 13–14 hour day, most women did not regard themselves as victims. Instead, they saw themselves as strong and capable; many took pride in their ability to earn wages *and* take good care of their families (Heitlinger, 1996).

Non-marriage or voluntary childlessness met with a high degree of social disapproval; it was better to be divorced than never-married (Šiklová, 1993). The majority married very young: the modal age for women was 18–20 years, and for men 21–22 years. By the age of nineteen, 27–30 per cent of Czech women were married, and by twenty-one more than half (52–58 per cent). As the Czech demographers Milan Kučera and Blanka Fialová (1996, p. 14) argue,

this marriage 'democratization' was reflected in higher incidence of divorce. A large number of marriages were entered into after a brief acquaintance; a frequent incentive was the pregnancy of the bride (at the end of the 1960s almost one half, at the end of the 1980s almost 55 per cent of first children were born from premarital conceptions). Entering marriage was sometimes the first independent step undertaken by young people: high school or apprenticeship programs were often selected by their parents, the work placement was either officially determined, or, from the 1960s onwards, when there was more individual choice in this respect, this choice was typically strongly influenced by parents or personal connections.... Marriage thus often became the first independent step into adult life.

The communist housing policy favouring young married couples with children provided another incentive for women to marry and become mothers at a very young age. Fertility statistics reveal an extremely narrow age distribution: one-third of all women gave birth to their first child before reaching the age of 21 years, and one-half before 23. Second children usually followed two years later. The average age at the birth of first child was 22, and of the second 24. In contrast, in Western Europe the average age of women at first birth was 26–27, an average reflecting a much broader range of ages. Eighty per cent of Czech women gave birth to at least one child by the age of 26, and by the age of 30, only 10 per cent remained childless. Fertility was, none the less, below or barely at the replacement level. Few women had more than two children, and the one-child family was quite common (Lesný, 1978; Heitlinger, 1987; Kučera, 1994: Kučera and Fialová, 1996).

Abortion rather than contraception was the major method of birth control. Czech researchers estimate that every third pregnancy was aborted. An examination of demographic characteristics (age, marital status and parity) reveals that Czechoslovak abortion rates peaked among married women with two children over the age of twenty-five, while in the West the most rapid growth of abortions has been among young childless single women (Heitlinger, 1987, pp. 146–57). As Kučera and Fialová (1996, pp. 22, 23) argue,

the main cause of the high incidence of abortion **was an almost total absence of use of contraceptives**. Hormonal contraception was for a long time regarded as harmful to women's health. The availability of abortion discouraged interest in preventing unwanted conceptions. [emphasis as original]

While Czech women generally had only the number of children they wanted, the realities of their daily lives were quite grim. Women suffered from stress and exhaustion caused by 13–14 hours day (including 4 or 5 hours devoted to domestic work), discrimination in the workplace, and lack of leisure. These experiences led many to reject the goal of women's equality itself. Such attitudes were reinforced by the fact that women's paid employment and equality were chosen as goals not by women themselves but were imposed on them by the communist party-state (Wolchik, 1992).

THE VELVET REVOLUTION AND THE POSTCOMMUNIST TRANSITION, 1989–

The postcommunist transition was initiated by the November 1989 anti-communist Velvet Revolution, the subsequent collapse of the communist regime, and the election in June 1990 of the reformist Civic Forum government. As in other former communist countries, 'the lifting of the communist lid over the boiling cauldron has fully revealed the existing conflicts between nations and states in the region. The Czech–Slovak controversy has resurfaced although its character is very different from that of the prewar republic' (Wandycz, 1992, p. 271). The June 1992 general elections revealed profound and, as it turned out, irreconcilable differences between Czech and Slovak approaches towards economic, social and constitutional reforms. On 1 January 1993, the country was peacefully divided into two independent states – the Czech Republic and Slovakia.

Elected on a platform advocating rapid move towards a free market economy, the new Czech government headed by the well-regarded economist Václav Klaus made large-scale privatization of property in all sectors of the economy, including health care, its top priority. None the less, the legal–administrative framework of the privatization process has remained under the control of the central authorities, as has, to date, the allocation of the total resources available to health care (Heitlinger, 1995).

Implications of Czech Postcommunism for Health Care and Nursing

The Velvet Revolution brought to an end the socialist experiment in 'free' health care. Since the Velvet Revolution, pressure has been mounting to make changes in the health care system as quickly as possible, and a complete reorganization of the 'public service' model of health care is currently under way. Mandatory health insurance and privatization of health care emerged as the two key measures of the postcommunist health care reform. Various forms of health insurance were suggested – but, in the end, the reformers picked a fee-for-service scheme covering all types of health services (including dental and nursing care), facilities, and prescription drugs. Privatization was initially viewed as merely one instrument in a broader framework of co-ordinated reform measures, but since the election of the first Klaus government in June 1992, it came to be seen as one of the ultimate goals of the health care reform.

However, salaries of health care personnel have remained low, barely keeping up with inflation. In 1994, the average salary of 'middle level' health care personnel was 6896 Kč (US $265) a month. However, without additional bonuses for overtime, shift work, night work, and work on weekends and during public holidays, the average salary would have been 17 per cent lower, that is only 4367 Kč ($168). The starting nursing salary was much lower than the average, just over 3000 Kč ($115) (Riebauerová, 1995).

Many nurses, including the majority of our informants, have responded to low pay and stressful work conditions on an individual basis, by leaving for other jobs. The exit has been most pronounced in Prague, particularly in hospitals located on the outskirts of the city. Some of these, such as the Motol Hospital, had already experienced nursing shortages during the communist period (Emingerová, 1989). Since the Velvet Revolution, Prague's economy has been booming, creating many new employment opportunities with better pay and working conditions. In 1992, Thomayer Hospital in Prague was short of 25 nurses, while Motol Hospital was short of seventy nurses. By 1995, Motol's shortage grew to more than 160, although the Ministry of Health has disputed this claim (HC, 1992; 'Ministr Rubáš chce prověřit nemocnici Motol', 1995; 'Rubáš o platech', 1995).

As we noted, young and inexperienced nurses were already leaving for other jobs in significant numbers during the communist period. Those who are leaving today include many 'experienced older nurses for whom work in the existing conditions has become unbearable' (Mellanová, 1993, p. 3). Nurses are leaving to establish their own businesses, such as home care agencies or, in one highly publicized case, an 'erotic saloon' set up by a former Motol hospital nurse. Others are leaving for jobs with higher pay and less responsibility in banks, health insurance firms, and boutiques, or are temporarily moving abroad (McClune, 1995).

As a 'buffer zone' country,[4] the Czech Republic, located in the heart of Europe at the crossroads between East and West, has become both an exporter and importer of nurses. Since dismantling the once formidable border crossings with West Germany and Austria – which during communism were policed by watch towers, dogs and armed guards – Czech (and Slovak) citizens can now travel freely to neighbouring countries. The initial fear that open borders would unleash a flood of migrants from the (relatively) impoverished Czechoslovakia to the economically prosperous Germany and Austria has not materialized, although a significant number of people commute regularly across the border for work. Some, especially young people, leave for extended periods of time. At the same time, the growing prosperity of the 'buffer zone' countries is attracting migrants from further East.

The strikingly disparate levels of income and unemployment create strong incentives for this type of labour migration. Wages in 'buffer zone' countries are approximately one-tenth of those in the neighbouring countries to the West, while prices are about one-fifth, though rising. The ratio between wages in the 'buffer zone' countries and those further East is also 1 : 10. In 1994, average wages in the Czech Republic were approximately $220 ($250 in Prague) per month, compared to $10–15 per month in the Ukraine. Czech unemployment in 1993 was only 3.5 per cent, compared with 17 per cent in Croatia, 16 per cent in Bulgaria, 15 per cent in Poland, and 14 per cent in Slovakia (Wallace and Palyanitsya, 1995; Wallace *et al.*, 1995). Labour migrants are therefore pulled westwards. The migrants tend to come on both long-term or short-term contracts.

The 'domino effect' of labour migration is also evident in nursing, although numbers of migrants have so far been quite small. Since 1991, several private agencies from Germany and Austria have been actively recruiting Czech nurses on short-term contracts. The salaries offered have been typically below those earned by German and Austrian nurses, but on average five times higher than the going rate in the Czech Republic. The typical migrant nurse is young and single, although there have been cases of older married nurses who have left their children behind with relatives (McClune, 1995). The necessity to learn German further restricts the pool for whom work abroad is an attractive option ('O Rakousko je jen malý zájem', 1993).

Just as Czech migrant nurses typically work as nursing assistants or aides (as our respondent Petra did), nurses from the Ukraine and Bulgaria tend to perform such auxiliary work in Prague hospitals (Heitlinger's interview with the Director of Nursing, teaching hospital in Prague, May 1995).

Changing Orientations towards Marriage, Birth Control and Motherhood

Although there were 9000 more marriages in 1990 than in 1989, this was only a temporary blip caused by the phasing out of the communist pronatalist programme of low interest loans for young married couples. Since 1990, the number of marriages has declined consistently, by a whopping 11 per cent between 1992 and 1993, and by an additional 4 per cent between 1994 and 1995, despite a favourable age structure. As the absolute number of marriages decreased, and the range of ages at first marriage broadened, the average age at first marriage increased, from 21.4 years in 1990 to 23.2 years in 1993 (Pavlík *et al.*, 1995, pp. 12–18). This figure is expected to increase much more rapidly within the next few years as the young people who have postponed their marriages decide to get married (Kučera and Fialová, 1996, p. 47).

The decline in marriages has been accompanied by a similar decline in the birth rate. There were 109 300 fewer children born in 1994 than in 1990, a decline of 9 per cent. The fertility decrease has been most pronounced among women aged 20–24: during 1990–3, fertility for this age group declined by 17 per cent (Pavlík *et al.*, 1995, pp. 28–9). With new employment opportunities opening up, and the price of housing and childcare soaring, many young people are postponing the onset of marriage and parenthood from their early to mid-20s or even later. It is too early to say whether some women will choose to avoid marriage and/or motherhood altogether.

Women are also adopting different strategies towards birth control, moving from abortion to contraception. The total number of abortions declined by 57 200 between 1990 and 1994, while the number of women using birth control pills has tripled since 1991. The incidence of abortion in 1993 was 26 per cent lower than the previous year, although it remains high by Western standards (Kayal, 1994; Pavlík *et al.*, 1995, pp. 33–40, 1996, pp. 31–7; Kučera and Fialová, 1996, pp. 76–80). Unlike Poland, the reduction in abortion has been achieved without the imposition of restrictive legislation.

Thus postcommunist reproductive behaviour has been characterized by both continuities and discontinuities. As Kučera and Fialová (1996, pp. 50, 65, 68) argue,

> the proportion of first children born within 8 months after marriage increased from 42% in 1989 to **56% in 1994**. The marital behaviour of some sections of the young population therefore did not change, and still corresponds to the model of the 1980s, when marriages were entered into at a young age only after a conception. That is why even with such a pronounced decline in the total number of marriages the average age at first marriage increased only very slightly. . . .
>
> The fertility of couples who prior to 1993 did not postpone marriage remained almost the same, which means that they did not postpone childbirth either. These couples were therefore behaving **traditionally** (in the postwar sense) – they continued to have children during the first few years of marriage, but they also completed their fertility very early. . . .
>
> A complete reversal of previous tendencies occurred in 1992 and especially in subsequent years, when the decline in the intensity of marital births according to [mother's] age and birth order meant a pronounced gradual decrease in birth frequency, **at first of only first-born children, but in 1994 also of second children**. [emphasis as in original]

The increasing diversity in marital and reproductive behaviour is clearly captured in our small sample, which includes women of roughly the same age who married and had their first child very young, women who are now divorced, and women who have deliberately postponed marriage and motherhood. Our interviews offer no indication that Czech women are beginning to subscribe to Western ideologies expounding the advantages of a 'child-free lifestyle'. Rather, they reflect numerous patterns of reconciling traditional marriage patterns with the reality of postcommunist society. The full variety of these strategies can be found on the following pages, and will be analysed in the final chapter of this book.

NOTES

1. Prior to 1969, when Czechoslovakia became a federal republic, there was only one national ministry of health.
2. Eighty per cent of nursing graduates obtained their qualifications from these high school programmes. The remainder met the requirements of a nursing diploma in special two-year nursing courses for high school graduates.
3. However, as the Czech émigré sociologist Mita Castle-Kaněrová pointed out to Alena Heitlinger in a private communication, the analysis of the family under communism as a 'free zone' where people can resist 'the intrusion of the communist party-state' is too general and simplistic. The role of the family was more ambivalent. On the one hand, it was a sphere of privacy and escape, but on the other, the 'escape' was to some extent manipulated. In many respects, the private isolated family, composed of atomized individuals retreating into their privacy and splendid isolation, was exactly what the communist political elites wanted.
4. Claire Wallace *et al.* (1995) from the Central European University define the 'buffer zone' as a geographic area between Eastern and Western Europe. 'Western Europe' is comprised mainly of countries belonging to the European Union (EU), while the 'buffer zone' consists of countries on its eastern rim which have been the objects of integration and stabilization by the EU through various aid programmes and association agreements. This category includes Poland, Hungary, the Czech and Slovak Republics, and to a more limited extent Romania, Bulgaria and the Baltic States. 'Eastern Europe' forms a zone of its own, and includes countries of the former Soviet Union such as the Ukraine, Belarus, Russia, Moldova and the Caucasian region. Levels of income and economic development vary considerably, both within and between these zones, steadily improving as one moves from the East to the West.

REFERENCES

Emingerová, Dana (1989), 'Motol volá SOS', *Mladý svět*, 20–26 June.

HC (1992), 'Sestř ičky odcházejí za lepším', *Statim*, 30 September.

Hauser, Eva (n.d.) *About the Perspectives of Feminism in Czechoslovakia* (Prague: Curriculum Centre and Library for Gender Studies).

Havelková, Hana (1993a), '"Patriarchy" in Czech Society', *Hypatia*, **8**(4), pp. 89–96.

Havelková, Hana (1993b), 'A Few Prefeminist Thoughts', in Nanette Funk and Magda Mueller (eds), *Gender Politics and Post-Communism. Reflections from Eastern Europe and the Former Soviet Union* (New York and London: Routledge), pp. 62–73.

Heitlinger, Alena (1979), *Women and State Socialism: Sex Inequality in the Soviet Union and Czechoslovakia* (London: Macmillan Press/Montreal: McGill-Queen's University Press).

Heitlinger, Alena (1987), *Reproduction, Medicine and the Socialist State* (London: Macmillan Press; New York: St Martin's Press).

Heitlinger, Alena (1993), 'The Impact of the Transition from Communism on the Status of Women in the Czech and Slovak Republics', in Nanette Funk and Magda Mueller (eds), *Gender Politics and Post-Communism. Reflections from Eastern Europe and the Former Soviet Union* (New York and London: Routledge), pp. 95–108.

Heitlinger, Alena (1995), 'Post-Communist Reforms and the Health Professions: Medicine and Nursing in the Czech Republic', in T. Johnson, G. Larkin and M. Saks (eds), *Health Professions and the State in Europe* (London and New York: Routledge), pp. 213–27.

Heitlinger, Alena (1996), 'Framing Feminism in Post-Communist Czech Republic', *Communist and Post-Communist Studies*, **29**(1), pp. 77–93.

Kayal, M. (1994), 'Eroding an Abortion Culture. Causing a Drugstore Revolution, Contraceptives are Changing the Lives of Czech Couples', *The Prague Post*, 20–26 April.

Kemény, István (1982), 'The Unregistered Economy in Hungary', *Soviet Studies*, **34**(3), pp. 349–66.

Kučera, Milan (1994), *Populace České republiky 1918–1991* (Praha: Česká demografická společnost/Sociologický ústav Akademie věd České republiky).

Kučera, Milan and Fialová, Ludmila (1996), *Demografické chování obyvatelstva České republiky během přeměny společnosti po roce 1989* (Praha: Sociologický ústav).

Kumermann, Daniel (1996), 'If the Czech Catholic Church Harms itself, it Harms All of Society', *The Prague Post*, 8–14 May.

Legge, Michele (1996), 'Churches Seek Broader Role in Czechs' Lives', *The Prague Post*, 10–19 July.

Lesný, Ivan (1978), 'Plodnost poválečných kohort v ČSR', *Demografie*, **20**(2), pp. 106–16.

McClune, Emma (1995), 'Nurses Cross Border for Higher Salaries, Prestige', *The Prague Post*, 12–18 April.

Matějů, Petr (1992), 'Beyond Educational Inequality in Czechoslovakia', *Czechoslovak Sociological Review*, **28**, pp. 37–60.

Mellanová, Alena (1993), 'Dobrá vůle nestačí. O podmínkách ošetřovatelské péče v transformovaném systému zdravotní péče', *Sestra*, **3**(4), pp. 2–4.

'Ministr Rubáš chce prověřit nemocnici Motol' (1995), *Mladá fronta dnes*, 27 May.

'O Rakousko je jen malý zájem' (1993), *Lidové noviny*, 19 May.

Pavlík, Zdeněk *et al.* (1995), *Populační vývoj České republiky 1994* (Praha: Univerzita Karlova, Přírodovědecká fakulta, Katedra demografie a geodemografie).

Pavlík, Zdeněk *et al.* (1996), *Populační vývoj České republiky 1995* (Praha: Univerzita Karlova, Přírodovědecká fakulta, Katedra demografie a geodemografie).

Pekárková, Kateřina (1995), 'Czech Republic. More Liberty, More Hi-Fi Stereos, More Hatred', in Bernd Baumgartl and Adrian Favell (eds), *New Xenophobia in Europe*, European University Institute (London: Kluwer Law International), pp. 68–87.

Riebauerová, Martina (1995), 'Rubáš slíbil, že oddělení pro děti s leukémii se zavírat nebude', *Mladá fronta dnes*, 19 May.

'Rubáš o platech' (1995), *Večerní Praha*, 18 May.

Scott, Hilda (1974), *Does Socialism Liberate Women? Experiences from Eastern Europe* (Boston, MA: Beacon Press). Second edition (1976) renamed *Women and Socialism*.

Šiklová, Jiřina (1993), 'Are Women in Central and Eastern Europe Conservative?', in Nanette Funk and Magda Mueller (eds), *Gender Politics and Post-Communism. Reflections from Eastern Europe and the Former Soviet Union* (New York and London: Routledge), pp. 74–83.

Wallace, Claire and Palyanitsya, Andrii (1995), 'East–West Migration in the Czech Republic' (Prague: Migration Project, Central European University).

Wallace, Claire, Chmuliar, Oxana and Sidorenko, Elena (1995), 'The Eastern Frontier of Western Europe: Mobility in the Buffer Zone' (Prague: Migration Project, Central European University).

Wandycz, Piotr (1992), *The Price of Freedom. A History of East Central Europe from the Middle Ages to the Present* (London and New York: Routledge).

Wolchik, Sharon (1979), 'The Status of Women in a Socialilst Order: Czechoslovakia, 1948–1978', *Slavic Review*, **38**(4), 583–602.

Wolchik, Sharon (1981a), 'Demography, Political Reform and Women's Issues in Czechoslovakia', in M. Rendel (ed.), *Women, Power and Political Systems* (London: Croom Helm), pp. 135–49.

Wolchik, Sharon (1981b), 'Elite Strategy toward Women in Czechoslovakia: Liberation or Mobilization?', *Studies in Comparative Communism*, **15** (2–3), pp. 123–42.

Wolchik, Sharon (1992), 'Women's Issues in Czechoslovakia in the Communist and Post-Communist Periods', in B. Nelson and N. Chowdhury (eds), *Women and Politics Worldwide* (New Haven, CT: Yale University Press).

3 Monika

Monika and I met at a popular restaurant/bar in the city centre. At first, we had some trouble recognizing each other. When I first saw her she was chatting with the bartender and I assumed she was a friend of his. She looked like she was in her late twenties, not twenty-four, probably because she was heavily made up. Monika stared at me and looked away. Later she explained she thought I looked too young (I'd told her my age over the phone). Finally, since we were both obviously looking for someone, we approached each other.

The interview took place at the bar. At first, Monika's air of 'staginess' was almost overwhelming. With her impeccable clothes, poise, and assertive attitude, she evinces the overpowering, obviously cultivated, persona of a film star. (It's interesting that in the interview she states that she doesn't think of herself as a 'star' but she certainly came over that way.) Perhaps the most intriguing part of the interview was when she approached this subject head on and explained what beauty means to her. After the tape-recorder was turned off, the first thing Monika asked was whether I knew someone who could teach her English. Then she wanted to know who else I had interviewed from her class. When I made the passing remark that while most of the women in her class were married, the women from the year before her were mainly single, Monika laughed and said that the women in the other class were probably uglier.

Monika loves to talk, but isn't very interested in eliciting other points of view. She also has very fixed ideas about the United States, such as that the entire US is a bastion of liberalness. She spoke at length about a gay male American photographer she had interviewed for a television show. She was very supportive of gay rights and said that she didn't understand it when young Czech people expressed prejudice against gay men or lesbians. Such prejudice does not exist in the US, she suggested. She did not seem to believe me that not everyone in the United States has such open-minded attitudes.

Monika's primary question to me was when would I get married and did I want to have children? We discussed the complications of raising children and having a career. She was very surprised by how limited maternity leave provisions are in the US. She said she thought the US would be more advanced on these issues. She also stated that

if the United States decides to do something, the whole world tends to
change in accordance, and if two years later the US changes its mind,
the whole world has to reverse itself.

A few days later, one of Monika's classmates showed me a class
photo from when they were fifteen. I had trouble recognizing anyone,
except Monika. She was standing straight as an arrow, her long hair
falling perfectly into place, and staring directly into the camera with a
look that challenged it to capture her beauty. She still has that look
today.

I was born when my mother was nineteen. As I was growing up
she studied journalism and became a journalist. When we moved
to Prague when I was five, she started to work for Czech radio in
the foreign broadcasting department. I think she was very happy
with her job. Then she studied at university. I think she's made a
good career for herself.

How did she manage to combine her career with raising her
children?
Perfectly. She did it perfectly. She got her degree and I think it
took a lot of work, but there was never a moment that I or my
brother felt like we were missing out on something by her not being at home. It's like this – my mother never learned to ski, so
even if she had stayed at home, she would not have taught us how
to ski. So, it really doesn't matter. She didn't deprive us of anything important.

Do you think she ever wanted to stay at home?
Definitely not. She's very ambitious. She's very intelligent. She can
really go far if she wants to.

Did your father help out with the housework?
I have to say that my father is an unusual man because he doesn't
mind ironing or washing dishes. But he hates men's work such as
wallpapering or painting. I'm not saying he can't do it, it's just he
never does it as well as he does the laundry. I have to admit that
to this day he'll do my ironing.

When you were fifteen or sixteen, did you have any ideas about what you would be doing now when you're twenty-five?
I had some plans with a friend who got killed in a car accident. We were best friends and we would have two apartments. One we would rent out. In the other we would live together and enjoy ourselves. As far as having a profession is concerned, we did not think about that. Our main goal was to enjoy life. What's going to happen in the future did not weigh too heavily on us. And I think I have retained this outlook to this date.

Why did you decide to study nursing?
I was inclined to study the humanities, but when I had to chose a secondary school, I looked down the list and thought: teaching – I'm not interested in that; regular academic high school (the so-called *gymnásium*) – that's horrible, full of idiots; agriculture – ugh; secretarial college – what a terrible thing to spend all day behind a desk. But nursing high school – I thought I am socially minded enough for this. There was just nothing else. I thought I would enjoy it, and I was glad to go. I was convinced that I would be able to help people. I was 14 years old.

What did you think of it as a job?
I never worked as a nurse. It's a complicated story, but when I started school I was hit by a strong case of adolescent rebellion. I decided I didn't want to go to school after all. I thought everyone is stupid, including the teachers and my parents. Just the idea of listening to them!

So I arranged to fail a few courses. If I'd failed only two subjects, I would've had to redo my exams right after the summer vacation. But with three Fs, I wouldn't have to spend the whole summer studying – I knew my mother would make me retake the exams if I were able to – and I would leave school.

So I stopped studying. I failed that whole year but my mother said I had to stay in school, I had to get a high school diploma. She would not let me enrol in an apprenteship programme or go straight to work. So I ended up repeating the first year. But by then I'd calmed down and things were much easier. As time went on, we studied more academic subjects I found interesting and was good in.

But I wanted to explain why I never worked as a nurse. In my fourth year at school, when I was 18 years and 2 months old, I was in a very bad car accident. There were three of us in the car – a guy, my friend and I. The boy was driving and crashed. My friend was dead on the spot. It took me 3 months to recover – a month and a half in the hospital and a month and a half at home, under the care of a rehabilitation therapist.

The school principal was incredibly helpful and arranged for me to graduate even though I didn't have the requisite hours of practical experience. So I graduated, but with my doctor's warning that for two years I couldn't gain any weight, have children, or have a demanding job. But to be a nurse you have to be prepared to stand on your feet for 7 hours straight. Since I couldn't do this, I was given another exemption. Usually you need to work as a hospital nurse for at least a year before you can work in a polyclinic. But I was able to start right away at the polyclinic. For the most part, I worked in administration.

What kind of work do you do now?
I am a TV journalist. I won an anchor competition – a camera test and a voice test – and I've been doing it for about half a year now. I do primarily publicity, various news stories, or cultural events. I have to say I am completely satisfied with my job, but I'm not sure that I'd want to do it my whole life. I've just recently started moderating live programmes and my supervisors are happy with my work. I myself can't be objective – I think I look awful when I watch it. I think to myself, 'Oh no, that didn't work out.' But my supervisors are very happy.

It's work with people and it's interesting, so maybe I have satisfied my original aims. But it's too early to say.

Are you married?
No.

Are you in a serious relationship with anyone?
I'm dating someone, but it's not serious.

Do you want to have children someday?
Of course.

What do you think is a good age to have your first child?
There are two views on that – the medical and mine. The medical experts say that presently in the Czech Republic, it's best for a

woman to have children early because of the environmental problems here. Having children early lowers the risk of illness or miscarriage.

But from my perspective, as a young woman, I think 28 is the best age. But I told myself I would wait until I feel some maternal instinct within myself, until I feel like I really want a child. Until I need a child. I wouldn't want to have an unwanted pregnancy and be forced to have a child. At my age I would probably never decide to have an abortion. I am old enough to be a mother and I'd hope I'd never get pregnant with someone I don't care enough about to have a child with.

What is your opinion of abortion?
It's an individual's choice.

Should there be any laws governing it?
No. Under no circumstances. On the other hand, I would support a law that certain people should be sterilized, such as the mentally ill. That's because they have very strong sexual urges. If you get two mentally ill people of the opposite sex together, you can't stop them. So I think they should be required to be sterilized so they can't reproduce – they will only reproduce another simpleton like them.

But otherwise there shouldn't be any restrictions on abortion?
No, none at all. I think it's clear from the examples of Poland or Ireland that women who get pregnant and know that they cannot have another child, have illegal abortions and risk their lives. Or they go abroad and have them.

I really strongly believe there should be no laws restricting abortion. The only people who want such laws are women who can't have children, feminists, and men who don't understand this issue.

Why feminists?
I don't know, I get that feeling from them. . . . Maybe I didn't say that right. It's just I met one like that. I was very surprised because I'd expect a feminist to leave the choice up to women. Maybe I shouldn't have generalized. I only met one who thought that way. Because she couldn't have children she was very extreme. She didn't give away compliments to men, but when it came to abortion, she was resolutely against it.

What do you think are the best and the worst aspects of not having children?
Right now in my life? The best part is that I am not bound to anyone or responsible for anyone. Having a child requires taking responsibility for them. If I had a child it would've been even harder to arrange a time for this interview. With a child there are many limitations on one's life, time-wise I mean. But of course the child makes up for this in many ways. It must be nice to see who you've given birth to growing up and calling you 'mom'.

When you have children do you want to stay at home with them?
Of course, but just for a limited time.

How long?
It depends on money, but as long as I can afford it, until they are past first grade. Until they are about seven. I'd be with them, but they'd also go to kindergarten, but not for the whole day. It's not good for children to be in kindergarten from seven to five, but it's not good for them to be at home all day either. I'd put them into a pre-school that focuses on teaching English. This way they meet other children and they can start learning. I think it's important to pay a lot of attention to the child's first experiences at school. If they don't like it at the age of six, then how will they like it after that?

Would you like to continue working while you raise your children?
Depends on the job. I could still work at the TV station. Why not when the child is in kindergarten? Or I could study a foreign language or something. I definitely wouldn't want to be just at home. I'd be very unhappy. That's why I'd put the child to school to have some time to myself. I hope I'll marry a responsible decent man who'll help me out in this.

What do you think it means to be a good father?
A good father – that's connected to being a good husband. He provides for his family. If there's one thing I don't want, it's to be in a position where I have to choose if I'll buy my child a banana or an orange. Or if she has to wear shoes that are too small for

her because I don't have enough money to buy her new ones. He has to be able to provide for us – not millions, but enough that money is not a problem. I know people say that money is not important, but money brings freedom.

What would you say if your family could live off only your income and your husband suggested he stay at home and you go to work. Would you agree?
It would depend on my job. There's work and there's work. Some jobs demand 14 hours days, some only 4–5 hours a day. But I wouldn't want to miss the best years with my child when I really want to be with him. When I have him, I want to enjoy him. So of course, I'd want to stay at home.

Do you think a man can raise a child as well as a woman?
Of course. Why not? A lot of men are better parents than mothers.

What's your opinion of day-care centres?
I was in one and I don't think it hurt me. I was always very energetic. It never hurt me. Or maybe I can't judge if it hurt me or not. But it was probably a good thing because otherwise I would've been too much to handle at home.

In any case, I understand why women have to put their children into day-care. But as soon as they can afford to stay at home with them, it's much better for them to do that.

Do you live with your parents?
Yes. My parents are divorced, but still live together. My brother lives there too.

Of course I'd like to have my own apartment, but that's impossible right now. Sometimes I'm annoyed at living at home since I'm already twenty-four. My mother will always be my mother and will always worry about me. So if I go out at night, she can't sleep until she sees me safely back home. That gives me a bad conscience.

But on the other hand, there are certain advantages. I don't need to cook. When my parents were away and I was working, I didn't have time to go shopping so I had no food. This doesn't happen when my parents are at home. And it's cheaper to live at home. But of course, if I got a reasonable offer on an apartment, I'd leave to live on my own.

Does your mother do most of the housework?
We split it in half. I have to say I don't enjoy cooking. I know how, but I don't enjoy it. My mom loves to cook and she cooks well. But of course, when she's tired, I'll cook. Otherwise we split the cleaning – my mom, my dad, and I. My brother doesn't help out because he's sixteen and he is quite impossible. If it was up to him, we'd be under metres of dust. You tell him to do something, he says that he will do it, but 14 days later it's still not done.

Who do you think should do the housework?
Who should do it? A maid. If I could afford it, I'd get a maid. I definitely wouldn't wash the windows or the curtains. The basic cleaning up I'd do myself. I don't think I would enjoy hiring somebody for every chore. It's of course quite different if you have a small apartment than if you have a house. I don't think I could manage a two-storey house, if I ever manage to own one.

What do you think is the difference between how women live here and in America or France or England?
I'm lucky that I've travelled much of the world. I used to idealize the West. I thought everything there must be fantastic, that everybody is beautiful and has wonderful clothes. Then I went there and saw reality. Basically it's the same there as we have it here now.

Where have you been?
All over Europe and Asia, but not to America. But Asia is a completely different world. But to compare within Europe – French and German women are very ugly. It's disgusting. They have short legs so I can never buy pants there. But Germans in general are a dislikeable people. I hate their language. I'm sure that among them are some nice people, but as a nation, they strike me very negatively, especially with their nationalism. If another Hitler came there, the same thing would happen 50 years later. The people are like a herd of sheep. It's a horrible nation ... but to compare the women. It's often said that Czech women are the most beautiful in the world. French women have charm. So do Italian women, but it depends on what part of the country they are from.

It's the same here, except that a lot of women here still don't have the time and resources to take care of themselves as they do in other countries. There, women are raised to pay attention to themselves. For generations they've seen commercials and been told to buy creams for their faces. We didn't have that until six years ago. Here nobody knew what it meant to care for yourself. I don't want to say they didn't wash themselves, but there was no attention paid to self-care – both inner and outer, spiritual and psychological. And that's where it comes from – all beauty comes from within. But we are just learning to cultivate this.

Those attitudes were not here before because . . .?
Because nobody taught them. To go to the hairdresser was considered a bourgeois act, because only a person who does nothing has time to spend looking good. A woman in a factory couldn't have a perm. They'd think she is lazy, doesn't work hard, and cares more about her appearance than her work.

In addition, they didn't have the products. I would love to own a cosmetics company, because it's guaranteed wealth. Look at the choices in products now! And at the influence of commercials. Every woman wants to be beautiful today and spends attention on herself. Those who have money invested in this will make a lot.

Why is it important to be beautiful?
It's not important to everybody. But to me it's important. Everyone is beautiful in a different way. I've never seen an ugly woman. It's a matter of fixing yourself up. Then again I have a friend, a well-known make-up artist, who says this isn't true. That some women have the right features, and others do not.

In any case, for me it is important. I like beautiful people, beautiful places. But I'm not saying I judge people according to beauty. Or that I chose my friends that way. But it draws the eye. When I see a pretty girl and a pretty guy, it lifts my spirits more than if I see someone ugly. That's logical.

I want to go out into society and not look like some poor Cinderella. I'm not saying I make a star out of myself, but I care how I look. That means I go to the hairdresser, I make time to see a cosmetics consultant when I can. It's important to me, even for my work. At the polyclinic, this did not matter.

Is it more or less important for a woman than a man?
I don't think it should be more important to women. Women think beauty is the most important thing. But you can have an ugly woman who is beautiful in other ways and guys go crazy over her.

It's the same with men. You have a beautiful-looking man, but you can tell he is narcissistic and you shouldn't waste time on him. Then you have a guy that doesn't look like much, but he attracts you.

Back to the comparison with Western women, do you think that they have more freedom than Czech women?
Definitely not. Today, definitely not. There's spiritual freedom and financial freedom. Money guarantees freedom. It's a means of being really free. It's fantastic if someone travels to Bali and meditates, but you need to have money to get to Bali. You need to have the means to realize your freedom. If you are a painter, but you don't have money and work as a boilerman, you aren't free anymore.

It's different for everyone. There are people who can be free behind bars. Everyone has an inner freedom. You may never find it. Your whole life people may think you are free, that you have everything, but you don't feel that way. It's very individual.

How has your life changed since the revolution?
For me, not at all. Only that I can travel.

I was seventeen when the revolution occurred. I lived at home and had to listen to my parents. I wasn't affected by the regime. I had my parents, I had enough to eat, life was good.

Who do you think has it better in life, women or men?
I think women, but it's very subjective. I'm happy I'm a woman. I wouldn't want to be a man. I'd have to do military service. But I think that in general your life is what you make it.

Does religion have any influence in your life?
No. I'm an atheist. I'm interested in reincarnation, hypnosis, psychoanalysis. But I think reincarnation is a kind of comforting belief.

When I was small, crying in bed, I asked myself what it will be like when I die. It was so horrible. I often cried because I couldn't imagine it. I just imagined nothingness. My heart was beating madly, I was very upset. From these memories of my childhood, I came to be interested in reincarnation. That fear of death is still with me today. I just can't imagine that I won't exist, but by then I wouldn't care. But the idea it's terrible, because I like life. I am hoping it will never be different.

I believe in fate, that it's predetermined what happens to a person. I'm very interested in numerology. I believe in fate, because otherwise I don't know how to explain that three of us were in that car and I lived and that girl died. Why? Who decided that? Did I have better luck? Luck means that my guardian angel, or whoever protects me, must be so worn out, because he has a lot of work with me. But he's doing a good job.

You take two people and the same thing happens to them both, but they take it completely differently. I'm very content with my life. But somebody else would be miserable because of it.

4 Magda

Magda and I met on Václavské náměstí, the central square in Prague, which is always teeming with shoppers, students, and what, at any given moment, seems like hundreds of American and German tourists. Perhaps the crowds swarming around us inspired her because within minutes of meeting each other, Magda declared how much she hates Americans and tourists, especially German tourists, because they drive the prices up. She quickly qualified her hatred of Americans to explain she hates all Americans, not just tourists. She expressed a very strong dislike of anything American and stated that she would never like to go to America. As she steered us towards a side-street cafe, she pointed to the fast food restaurants flanking the square and declared that the last place she would ever want to meet someone is in McDonald's.

Not surprisingly, the only question she asked of me was why as an American I have a Czech last name. She did not ask anything about the United States. Another member of her class who I later interviewed, seemed to know all about Magda's anti-American comments and described her as 'the woman who was very rude to you'. But if she meant to insult me with her anti-Americanisms, I found them much more amusing and right on target instead. Even when she is being sharply critical, Magda's approach and demeanour are very relaxed. She appeared to be someone who is very comfortable with life, not having to battle for what she wants to get, but who thinks it will just naturally come to her. This may come from the fact that she belongs to a high-profile family. She also gave the impression of having a fair amount of money.

Magda is extremely animated and has a very rich sense of humour. She often accompanies her jokes with hand gestures or by mimicking the voices of the people she is describing. And she really loves a good joke. After the 'official' interview was over, she returned to the theme of McDonald's and told me a story about a friend of hers who spent a few years in the US. On his return, all his friends secretly got together and put on T-shirts with American slogans and baseball caps. They went and 'suffered' the afternoon away, sitting in McDonald's. Meanwhile the man's girlfriend met him at the airport and was walking along through town with him when she said she had to go to the bathroom. They stepped into McDonald's and he came face to face with all of his friends sitting at the table, drinking Coca-Cola. His shock and amazement almost overcame the humour of the joke.

My parents are divorced, but my mother remarried soon after, so I have a step-father. My father then had a few women friends – you could say I had a number of stepmothers. But now he has a permanent partner.

How old were you when your parents divorced?
I was four. I was going to kindergarten.

Do you have any brothers or sisters?
It's a bit more complicated. From my mother and step-father, I have a seven-year-old sister. From my father and step-mother, I have a six-year-old sister. Plus my father's wife has a sixteen-year-old son. Now my step-father has also a thirty-year-old daughter, who has a three-year-old daughter. So it is all very complicated. I have a lot of siblings, but I don't know who belongs to me and who doesn't.

Where did your mother work while you were growing up?
My mother worked in a hospital as a secretary. Today she is a secretary at a company that sells medical equipment and pharmaceuticals. She started working there after spending the last seven years at home with my step-sister. We convinced her to go back to work because at home she'd go crazy.

Otherwise she would have still stayed at home?
Absolutely. Who wouldn't? But then again, now that my step-sister is going to school and isn't at home, my mother would soon get bored. It's good she went to work. She was always cleaning up and thinking up some more housework to do, silly things. But if it was up to her alone, she may have preferred to stay at home.

When you were growing up and she was working, how did she manage taking care of you?
When I was young my step-father was at home, because his time is completely his own. He is a painter, so he is always at home. My

mother worked in the building next door, so it was no problem for her to look in on me when she wanted to. My step-father is still at home, and now he takes care of my step-sister. He takes her to school and picks her up and takes care of things through the day before mom gets home.

Do you live at home?
Yes, I live with my parents, with my mother and my step-father and step-sister, and with a dog and some fish and a bird . . . there are lot of us!

It's comfortable to live at my parents'. I don't need to take care of anything. I just give them some money, and that's all. Everything is taken care of by my mother. If I come home from partying with my friends all night, my mother will tend to me the next morning, so I'm comfortable there.

Are you dating anyone seriously?
No, I'm not in a serious relationship. I have a number of good male friends, and one *especially* good friend, but it's not serious. He's a good friend, a very kind, trustworthy friend I can count on, who will help me no matter what happens. But it's not a serious relationship and that's nice, because I have time for other things, for my other interests and my other friends. I wouldn't say I even want a serious relationship, to have someone who'd always be watching me and to whom I'd have to dedicate all my time. . . . It's nicer to have someone like this and to also have time for my other friends. My friends and I often go to the mountains as a big group. It's better to go on such trips as a single person than with a partner, because whenever somebody brings their partner they watch who they smile at, who they talk to, who they fall asleep next to at night. So it's better to have a more open relationship.

Are you interested in ever getting married?
No. To tell the truth, I wouldn't mind if I never got married. I can live with someone and have kids, but it seems like a waste of time to get a piece of paper and have a big wedding for our thirty or so relatives. I want to have kids and a family, but not get married.

How many kids would you like to have?
I joke that I would like to have six, but I still don't have a father who will support them all! First I need someone who will support

us and take care of us. Probably two or three children is a reasonable number, but I wouldn't mind six. I like big families. But, I'd
like to wait because I'm helping raise both of my step-sisters –
they were born when I was 16 and 17 years old and I was always
helping to take care of them. So I want to enjoy some freedom
before I have my own kids.

When did you decide to go to nursing school?
When I was small. My mother worked in a hospital, so from a very
young age I was sure I would be a nurse. I wanted to be a midwife
or a birthing assistant, but I was talked out of that because I was
told it would be better to be a regular nurse and have a better
choice of jobs. I always wanted to be a nurse, so I studied nursing
– and then I never did it!

You never worked as a nurse?
No. I worked in a hospital while in nursing school, but that was
just for the obligatory clinical practice. I never worked during the
school holidays. My parents said I didn't need to work, I should
rest, so I didn't.

I always wanted to work in the ob/gyn ward, so I liked our clinical practice there. Then I was in surgery and internal medicine
wards, which I didn't like. It was hard work, especially psychologically. There were a lot of old people on these wards who were
dying, things like that. So I wasn't interested in nursing any more,
even though I did look for work after I finished school, until my
parents offered that I could stay at home.

So you finished nursing school and . . .?
I was home for one year. I was supposed to be taking English lessons, but I didn't go to classes very often, so I don't know any
English. Then I had an argument with my parents, and within three
days I started working. I took the first job I was offered, which was
a secretarial job. I liked it at first, but then it became very stereo-
typical work, because I was always picking up the phone and an-
swering one stupid question after another. Then I got tired of sitting
down all the time. I had to be there from 8:00 a.m. to 4:00 p.m.; I
couldn't leave. So I looked for something better and I found it.
Now I work as a nutrition counsellor. I do tests to check someone's
physical and nutritinal fitness. It's interesting because I get to travel
and meet new people.

How long have you worked there?
A year and a quarter, but I did some work there before I got this job. For a year I worked as a secretary, and at the same time helped out at the nutrition centre.

Do you have any future career plans?
Career? Absolutely not. I'm not the type. The only thing would be to study nutrition next year. A nutritional studies centre offering three-year courses has just opened in Brno. If I got accepted, I may want to do it. That's a possibility. It would help me in my work. But who knows what will be in a year?

If you could choose any of the following, what would you choose – the work you do now; any other job; studying at college; or being at home?
I certainly would not choose another job. Going to college – I'd have to consider that for a long time, and it would have to be something very interesting that I'd study. I think I'd like to stay at the job I have for few more years. If I did study, it would only be part-time, and only if I could keep this job.

It would be fine to be a housewife for about five years. If I now got pregnant and had to get married, I would like to be at home and take care of the child and of the housework, but I'm not planning it right now.

As long as I can, I'd like to keep this job. It's a good one even for somebody who has children, because there is a lot of free time. If I come in at eleven in the morning, nobody cares. If I leave at 2:00 p.m. in the afternoon and there are no tests to do, nobody cares. And I can take the work home if I want to. I can take the laptop home with me and work from home for a week if I want to.

Sometimes I decide I just want to take off skiing and that's fine. I decide I want to take off work on Wednesday, so on Tuesday morning I say, 'Listen boss, I want to go skiing' and he says, 'That's fine Magda, I'll take care of everything for you tomorrow.' You see, I have a boss who is a very kind person, a wonderful, smart man. He's a doctor, but he's no good at being a boss; he doesn't know how to hold the reins. People say that I'm the boss at work and he's the secretary. That makes it even easier to come to an agreement with him.

If you were 14 years old again, what kind of high school would you choose to attend?
There wasn't much to choose from, especially for girls, so nursing school was not such a bad choice for me. To go to a regular academic high school without going to a university and not have a vocation would be dumb. I wouldn't want to go to a secretarial school, that's boring. I wouldn't want to be a seamstress either. Then there are also those new fashionable management schools, but what do you do with that? Go on to college, which I wouldn't be good at. . . . Maybe I would study languages if somebody forced me to, but most likely I'd go back to nursing school. In addition to teaching me practical things I can use in my life or at home, nursing school taught me a new approach to people. It's hard to explain, but when a person is 15 and witnesses such suffering – when you see people die or go through difficult illnesses – and you talk to them . . . somehow you re-evaluate your ideas about life. It's different from studying at a regular high school and spending your time going to pubs with your friends. It was psychologically demanding, but I realized what is important to me – to be healthy and content rather than have a group of friends and a lot of money. Maybe it was also that at the time my mother was pregnant and gave birth to my step-sister. My mother spent lot of time in the hospital, so for a long time I took care of my sister alone. All of this came together to give me a sense of what I want and what I don't want from life, what is important to me. I definitely know that money and a high-salary career is not the most important thing for me. For me it's important to be content and healthy. It might sound clichéd, but when a person is not healthy and content, nothing can interest him. A person who is healthy, has a family whether their own or their parents' and siblings', who love her or him, that to me is important.

What do you think are the advantages and disadvantages of not having children?
Not to have children is very selfish. A childless person has time for herself, her interests, hobbies, work, and her partner, if she has one. But life without children, I would say, is sad. I have small siblings, so I can see that children are happy and playful. A person with children stays playful – to this day I can play like a small child. I build houses out of toy building bricks. My friends are the same, so when we go to the mountains we don't spend our time drinking. We play

a popular Czech game 'Don't be Angry', and also play cards and have fun. I think a person stays young when they have children.

I don't think you should have children when you're twenty though. You haven't lived long enough and you don't know very much. But if you have them later, then you can teach them from your experiences and thus raise the next generation. And I think it's good not to be alone in your old age. You have a partner, but perhaps with time your partner passes away. Say, if I find a husband who is ten years older than me, then I'll be sixty and he will be seventy, and he'll die and I'll be left alone without any kids and without my parents. Maybe I'll still have my siblings, but still, I think children liven up life. They also keep you busy. They always want to know something new so you have to find out about it. I think they keep you in touch with life. I simply can't imagine life without them.

Did you always plan on having them at a later age?
I don't know what I thought at fifteen or seventeen. I know I didn't want to get out of nursing school, and get married and have kids right away.

I think it's better to have children later. Twenty-five is a good age. But around thirty is ideal. I know from my mother and from my step-mother that when a person is older they enjoy their children more and spend more time with them. At twenty you are still a kid. You see your friends going out to the movies and having fun and you can't anymore. Then maybe you take it out on the children. Or you are so devoted to the children that you lose all your friends. So I think it's better to wait.

Who, in your opinion, should take care of a household in a family?
Here in the Czech Republic, it's customary that housework's mostly done by the woman. I think it should be split 50:50, based on who likes to do what. Definitely it should not be that the woman does everything. The wife used to have to go to work and take care of the home. Her husband would come home from work, pick up the paper and grab a beer, and sit in front of the TV. It definitely should not be like that.

I know how to do everything. I'm capable of doing all the housework, but I don't see why I should have to do that. It should be shared.

As long as the woman is a housewife then the larger part of the housework should be done by her, because that's her work. Then her husband should have room to earn a living and provide for his wife and children. But once they both work and they have kids, the housework should probably be split in half.

And should they share childcare?
Definitely. They should definitely split childcare. For the children it's important that they get care from both their mom and their dad. As long as the children are small, the mother can give them better care. But once they are bigger, their father can spend more of his free time with them. So while their mother is cooking, their father can take them out, or to the circus. I think there are some things that a woman does better than a man.

Such as?
Those smaller things like sewing, laundry, ironing. Cooking probably not. Men can do that just as well as women. But men are better at rougher work.

Probably that's how it was arranged a long time ago – that we are different, men and women. We were made for different things. Men for protecting the family, when they used to hunt. And women took care of the family. Today things are a bit different, but still I think women are better equipped to take care of the family.

I am not much of a feminist. I'd like to be at home and take care of the children. I'm definitely not the type to come home and say, 'Let's split the work in half.' If my husband supports me, I'll happily be at home. I don't like all that feminist talk about women being equal.

What does it mean to you to be a feminist?
From what I read in the papers, it's about women saying that they have to go to work and take care of the family and the children, that they have more work than men; that they don't have the same rights as men; that they have lower pay; and that everything should be equal.

But it is logical that a man should be paid more than a woman when it is he who supports his family. That's a very basic assumption.

What about if a woman is on her own?
Then that's another thing. You have to ask why she's on her own. I'm talking on the assumption that it's a normally functioning family. A woman alone – that's bad. But then why is she on her own? I

think that a person is always able to find some kind of partner who will suit them. If she's not able to do that, then that's her short-coming.

That kind of complete equality between men and women can never exist, because a woman can give birth and take better care of the children than a man.

Recently there was a debate on TV about feminism. Our whole family watched it and thought it was amusing. Everyone talked about how women are such poor things, that she has lower pay and when she goes to get a job, she doesn't have as good a chance as a man, because the employer assumes she will want to have children. But that's logical! It's logical to assume that a man supports his family so he should be paid more, under normal circumstances.

From the beginning, men and women have been different. It's that way with animals. The lioness takes care of the cubs and the lion hunts. It's a given with animals, and it's the same with people. Only now someone is trying to change it. Maybe earlier it was worse because women were supposed to go to work, have voting rights – I don't even need to have that.

What do you think it means to be a good mother?
A good mother . . . hmm. A good mother definitely spends time with her children, takes care of them, makes sure they are fed and materially provided for. She supports them in their interests. And she gives them a foundation at home that they can lean on, so whatever happens, whenever, they can return to her and know they have a home. Same thing with the father – it's exactly the same, even if a mom will always be a mom.

So a good father is the same as a good mother?
Exactly the same. He doesn't spend as much time with them when they are small. He's trying to make sure they are well-provided for. But when they are older, he should spend as much time as possible with them. It's not enough to just provide materially for them, especially when they are in puberty. There's plenty of cases where the father has no idea what the children are up to. Then suddenly he finds out his child is drinking or smoking pot, or his daughter is pregnant at age sixteen. 'How can this be!' he says. 'She had everything.' She had everything, but was afraid to go to her mother or father, because they would berate or wouldn't have time for her. That simply is the key – to have time for them.

Who in your household does most of the housework?
My mother and I. My father only does the shopping. We have a
very impractical father. He's a painter, but we do all the wallpapering,
house-painting, changing the light bulbs. Dad knows how to scramble
an egg and make a cup of tea, but that's about all.

**Do you feel any pressure from your relatives or from society in
general to get married and have kids?**
Definitely not from my parents. They're glad I'm single and have
time to take care of their kids. But sometimes my grandmother
does pressure me. She says 'My friends ask if you aren't strange,
not having two kids by the age of twenty-three.' I have a cousin
who is twenty-five and has two kids, so grandmother says to me,
'Karla has two kids and you don't even have a boyfriend!' I don't
have a serious boyfriend and at home the boys come and go like a
conveyor belt. I'm always getting calls from someone my parents
have never heard of. Now, when grandma hears that, she's at the
end of her rope. 'You're going to the mountains,' she says, 'and
who's going with you?' 'I don't know,' I say, 'three boys and four
girls . . .' 'Jesus Christ!' she says, 'You're going there alone with
three boys!' So yes, grandma does sometimes prod at me saying, 'I
hope I live long enough to see those grandchildren.' But there's
no way I'll get married and have kids just to please her. Not a
chance.

But my parents don't push me at all. My mother always says, 'At
your mother's, you feel best of all, don't you?' 'Of course,' I say,
'where would I rush off to?'

Plus, I won't have one of those grandmothers who'll take care of
my children if I have them now, because both my mother and step-
mother have young children of their own. My mother says, 'don't
count on me taking care of the grandkids when my child is grown,
I want to enjoy life.' My step-mother says she'll return the favour,
because I take care of her daughter. But I have to wait until they
want grandchildren and have time for them. I think that a grandmother is very important to a child. That's the person who spoils
them. I was spoiled by my grandmother because for years I was a
single child.

Who do you think has it better in life, men or women?
That's completely individual. It's completely up to me how I am
and completely up to the guy how he is.

Are you interested in politics?
To tell the truth, not very much. I know what's happening here and in the world, but I'm not interested in the details. After the revolution, when I was eighteen, nineteen years old, I would watch the TV news and read the papers. I was interested in all the changes. But I've realized it's possible to live without following all that. A person has a clearer mind that way than if they are always watching what goes on.

I go and vote when it's necessary, but I don't go looking for political involvement. I listen a lot to my parents in this. My father is very interested in politics and I trust his opinion.

To what extent did you change your plans for your life after the Velvet Revolution?
I would say I didn't change them at all. I didn't have any big plans. I'd say that in our family, basically our life didn't change following the revolution. My parents were constantly travelling abroad already before the revolution. My father was a freelance artist, it was always – there is money, there is no money. I have a commission or I don't. Because we could live normally, our lives didn't change.

Now it's harder for my father to get work. But then for me, I wouldn't have been able before to go from studying nursing to working at a nutrition centre. I would have had to work in a hospital – it was kind of pre-determined. But my personal plans haven't changed. I can travel without all the hassle, but that's about all.

Do you like to travel?
I do, if I have enough money. I need to have enough money to enjoy myself. I don't like to travel when I don't have enough for a decent meal. We used to hitchhike and sleep under bridges so it wouldn't rain on us. But we always had enough money that we could stay in a hotel if we wanted to.

I wouldn't want to go off to Italy and sit there counting my money to figure out if I can afford a whole pizza or only half. I simply must have enough to fulfil all my wishes when I travel.

I'm lucky in that I have a lot of relatives outside the Czech Republic. I often travel to Paris where I have a godmother. Whatever I thought of when I was there, whatever I wanted to see, I could see. So I wasn't like some Czech tourists, who have to count their money to see if they can afford to go to the Eiffel tower or not. If I saw something in a shop, then I knew I could afford to buy it.

Where would you go if you could travel anywhere?
Where would I go? Definitely not to America. I have a number of good friends who were there to work or to travel. They always came back disgusted by America.

My friend just came back from a visit and he said to us, 'Girls, I am so glad I am back. In the three days I've been here, I've seen more pretty girls than I saw for whole six months in America.'

I think we are different from Americans. I think we have tighter friendships. Or we did, maybe now it's changing.

I'd never go to America. I'm interested in New Zealand, South America, Asia. I'm interested in China because my uncle was an embassy representative there for four years, so I know a lot about it. He showed me photographs and told me a lot about it.

Or else I'd like to see Africa, or Italy where I haven't been. I'd like to drive through England. Or go to Russia, but it's dangerous and I'd be afraid to go there. Romania is interesting, but also too dangerous.

Maybe in time I'd like to see America, but only as a tourist to see the scenery, the countryside. I'd skip the big cities, because my friends have complained about them. If I had the chance I would definitely go there to look. But I'd definitely never want to live there.

5 Jana

Jana was interviewed twice, due to a tape malfunction that damaged the tape of her first interview. The second interview took place three weeks after the first. In the first interview, she spoke a great deal about her experiences as a nurse and her thoughts on the health care system. Like many of her classmates, she said that nursing is a very difficult job because it demands a lot of hard work, strange hours, and causes much psychological pressure. In return, a nurse receives low pay and little respect. She also said that she was troubled that doctors and nurses are often not responsive to patients' needs. Many of the nurses are very apathetic towards the patients. They are more interested in cleaning the sink than talking to the patients. She herself was always much more interested in finding out how the patient felt and talking to her/him, rather than cleaning up. This is why she left nursing and is now studying psychology. She also expressed concern over the transformation of the health care system and the difficulties among the poor in paying for health care.

She spoke at great length during the first interview about her religious beliefs. She defines herself as a Christian and considers Christianity an extremely vital part of her life. She is very open-minded, tolerant and curious about other systems of belief. In many ways she seems inclined towards 'New Age spirituality' in general, enjoying the atmospheres of some of Prague's 'alternative' tea houses – Hare Krishna restaurants, and the like.

Jana is a very casual and relaxed person. She doesn't dress up or aim to impress anyone. She takes discussions about social issues very seriously. She spent a lot of time reflecting over each question. She commented that it was helpful for her to have had three weeks to rethink her answers. She is also extremely generous and open-hearted, as was shown by her offer to devote another afternoon to the interview. In the end, the fact that the tape of our first interview was ruined ended up drawing us together, and allowing for a richer, more engaging discussion of the issues a second time.

Until I was six years old, I lived with both my parents. By the age of seven, I was living with two parents again, because my mother got divorced and remarried. So there was a gap of about a year.

Do you have any siblings?
I have five brothers. The youngest is twenty-nine, the eldest thirty-eight. All five are married and have families.

How old was your mother when you were born?
She was thirty-five. My father was thirty-eight.

Where did she work?
She worked for the Czech airline doing administrative work. She wanted to do something completely different. She wanted to be a teacher. She studied education and completed all her classes at the university, but she didn't finish her exams because her father didn't allow her to. Her father never wanted her to study and she didn't have enough strength to stand up to him. She went to classes behind his back. He found out and brought her back home. She had to commute to her classes, so he brought her home and guarded her. He didn't let her go anywhere. So she didn't finish. She was a bit soft and she let it go. She didn't think it was that important.

Why didn't he want her to study?
He wasn't against it on principle. He himself was a university professor. So was his wife. My mother had a brother and a sister, and not one of them was allowed to finish school. He wanted them to work and make money, not to study. My mother's brother finished college when he was older. Her sister finished high school but didn't go on after that. She works in some shop. And my mother had one exam left, but never finished it. I still don't understand why. And now she regrets it. She talks about it often, but that chance has passed. She got married soon after – she was very young, twenty or twenty-one when she got married and then she started working for the airline. She worked there for a long time and says she even enjoyed it. She's quite content there, just a times, when she encounters some problems, she regrets what happened.

So if she'd gotten a college degree and become a teacher, she would have made less money?
I don't know how it was before. But currently, if someone gets a degree, and doesn't have his own business or isn't doing something

like computers, then they have less money than someone who didn't go to college. That's the way it is here. You invest a number of years into your education, and then you make less money.

So doctors make less money than . . .?
Than construction workers. There is talk of raising their salaries, but it wasn't always thought of that way. Here workers, the working class, were really something! And college students were the spongers whom the workers had to support.

Do you think your mother ever wished to be a housewife?
She wouldn't have enjoyed it. She enjoys housework but she manages it alongside her work. She also needs contact with people. When she had me, she stayed at home for two years and than went back to work, because they didn't have enough money to support us all. About a week ago, she and I talked about how she regrets that she missed the years I was growing up and changing from week to week. If she could've, she would've stayed with me longer, until I was about four or five. But to be permanently at home – she wouldn't want that.

Did your father help out with the housework?
The first one, yes. The second one, not at all.
   The first one helped my mom wash the dishes or dust when he saw she didn't have time or wasn't feeling well. He was capable of doing all of her work – he could change our diapers, wash the windows or cook. He loved to cook.
   But my second father loves to garden. So whenever he can, he gardens – he cuts the grass, trims the fruit trees, digs. But at home when he sees that our mother can handle it all, he doesn't have a reason to help out.

How much time did your first father spend with you?
I don't remember. Not at all. But from what I hear, I know it was not a lot. My mother was usually with us alone. Dad stayed at work and went out with his friends, things like that. He'd come home very late so he didn't spend a lot of time with us. When we went away on weekends to the cottage, he'd be with us. I think he quite likes children, I can see it in the good relationship he now has with with my nephew, for instance. But I think then he was too young, and he just didn't spend time with us.

And your other father?
He does. He would come home from work and – as long as he wasn't mowing the lawn – he'd talk to me, tell me what his life was like as a boy. He's from a small village in Moravia, so I would always laugh at his stories. He told me riddles and carried me around the apartment on his back. I loved that.

When did you decide to go to nursing school?
When I was eleven or twelve. My second father was a doctor, so I would go visit him in his office. I really like it there. My brother wanted to be a doctor. We don't have any other relatives who are doctors, but we both were drawn to it. So at about ten or eleven, I decided I wanted to be either an actress or a nurse. I signed up for the arts high school as my backup in case I didn't get into nursing school, which was where I really wanted to go.

When you were fourteen, what did you think you'd be doing at your age now?
I had no idea, I didn't think about it very much. I thought that at this age I'd be working in a hospital and be married and that was about it. But I wasn't very interested in thinking about it.

And now things are different?
Well, I'm not married and I don't work in a hospital anymore, even though I still consider returning to nursing, because I miss it.
Now my plans are to travel in order to learn a foreign language and have some experience. I'd like to finish college. I'd like to return to the hospital because I miss the work and I miss the people. So maybe when I finish college, I'll get some short-term work in a hospital. But after that I don't know what I want to do. I also now think that twenty-five is not the boundary line when I have to get married. I think a little differently now. I see that I have time. I could get married closer to thirty, that's not a problem. Marriage is also not the end station. I am not just waiting for someone to marry. There are a lot of things I can do. I can travel, and I can see things.

To what extent did your ideas about life change following the Velvet Revolution?
They changed, if only in that I can travel or go and work abroad if I want. I can do this without the problems there used to be. Right now, I am supposed to go to Germany to work with an organization

for handicapped people. Before I couldn't have done that, unless I had connections or lots of money and even then it was difficult. Now anybody who wants to can travel.

I also have the opportunity to go to school in my thirties and forties. I'm not limited by my age: being under twenty-five, studying and then getting a job, as it was before. So I have a lot more opportunities to improve myself. I can even study privately now.

I used to have piano lessons at a conservatory. When it was clear I was not going to go on and become a professional pianist, the lessons stopped. Now I could be fifty and decide I want to have lessons!

There are now many more opportunities to develop myself and generally learn things. I can meet new people. I can meet foreigners like you. I am discovering life, new people and how people live elsewhere. So I discover that people in Australia are just like me, they're not any different even though they are way out on the map.

What was the work like in the hospital?
It was interesting. What I didn't like was that there wasn't enough time. None of the doctors were able to spend time with us to tell us what they were doing and why, what the drugs were for.

Ideally, the head of the department, or any one of the other doctors, should take the nurses aside and tell them what the diagnoses of all the patients are, what new drugs are available, and so forth. There should always be new information, more learning. But there was no time for that. There wasn't time to eat lunch, much less to sit down and talk about something. Even if the nurses made time for it during their time off, the doctors didn't. We were continually doing new things or using new drugs and even if we asked about them, the information was never complete. It was interesting work, because it was a small surgery ward and there were a lot of special operations going on, which I got to see. But there was never enough time.

At that time, when I was eighteen, it didn't bother me that much that there wasn't time to explain everything. I had what I needed, I lived with my parents. It didn't even occur to me that I could do something different or that I could go somewhere to study or go away for a longer period of time. I was raised to think that I would finish school and get a job. There was no chance that I could take a year off school and go and travel somewhere. I'm sure a lot of people did it, but it never occurred to me.

I didn't consider going to a university. I realize now that it was partly because I didn't have enough self-confidence. I still don't, but it's better now. I thought I wasn't good enough. I have an older brother who is very talented at everything. I grew up in his shadow. He knew how to paint, he played the piano, he sang. In comparison to him, I didn't have a chance. How could I go to university when Petr went? Now I think differently. Even though I know that I'm not like him, I know that everybody can do something and I can at least try.

But then I thought that I'd finish high school, get a job, and that's that. That I started realizing that it doesn't have to be that way. And it felt horrible to stop learning, to be stunted at eighteen.

Maybe I'm a little bit vain, but it bothered me when the doctors treated us like cleaners. We had a lot of work, but we did do janitorial work, because there were no cleaners. It bothered me not to get any respect, not to have my work given any regard. Because the work should be respected. I don't think physicians should be superior. But, I wanted the doctors to treat us as equals and tell us what they knew. Of course, there are a lot of things we wouldn't have understood, but if they explained it even partially.... There were a lot of things I'd ask about and the doctor would say, 'you wouldn't understand that'. And that was it. So we were held back.

Later, some baccalaureate programmes for nurses were created, but then I'd already left. I had some friends who were in college and I realized that there were other places where I could ask a question and actually learn something. I went to study psychology because it had always interested me.

The first year was the best because my head was full of what I wanted to learn. It was wonderful. Very interesting. Then, of course, I started getting used to it, so it wasn't that exciting anymore. But it's still an interesting topic that has opened a whole new world for me.

If you were fifteen again, what would you study?
Probably nursing school. Maybe I'd change my mind and go to the academic high school to improve my overall education. We didn't, for example, study geography. We had history, but only for two years. Biology we had for only one term. So I guess I'd go to an academic high school so I could learn all these basic things.

Now they are considering changing it so that you'd go to nursing school after going to a high school. You'd graduate from nursing school at twenty-one or twenty-two. At fourteen or fifteen very few people know what they want to do. Even at 18 people have trouble deciding. How can you at fourteen?

At the age of fourteen, I went a number of times to watch dissections. I saw dead bodies being opened up. At fourteen it really changed me. At that age you are still almost a child and suddenly you see horrible wounds. In nursing school when I was fifteen, sixteen, seventeen, I met people who were dying. At such an age, as long as one of your relatives doesn't die, you don't even think about such things. It was very difficult.

I don't regret it. I'm glad I could see it so soon in life. It cleared up a lot of things for me. But it's probably better if you see it when you're eighteen and know what you are getting into. Then you realize that you are going to go into a hospital where there will be people who need your help and who maybe are dying. But a 14-year-old child thinks, 'in nursing school I don't have to do math'.

How many children would you like to have?
I'd like to have four of my own, if it's financially possible. I'd also like to adopt a child, but probably only one.

What would you like to do if you have children?
I'd like to be with them as long as possible. But I don't know what would be best for them – for me to stay with them until they go to school at the age of six, or for them to spend at least a year in kindergarten. It may also depend on if I had people around me with children in the same age group. If I did, then sometimes the children could get together, because children need other children. I wouldn't want them to be sad, or to be afraid of other children. But in either case, I'd like to stay at home with them as long as possible so I don't miss out on the time they are growing up and I can give them the most of myself.

Do you care if you have boys or girls?
Not really. As long as they are healthy, it doesn't matter if they are boys or girls. But I'd prefer to have sons. At least one older son, then some daughters. I'd like to have at least one son . . . maybe I'd like to have more sons than daughters.

Do you think it's different to raise a girl than a boy?
I think it is. A girl can be really mischievous, or a boy can be mischievous, or both of them could be really good. It depends on

how they are raised. But when a boy grows up, he leaves home. He isn't as emotionally tied to his family. But a girl, even if she moves out, still comes back to her mother. So if a mother has a daughter, she isn't left all alone.

For example, even if I were to leave home, we have such a connection, that despite any differences, I could never put my mother in a home for the elderly. Even if we had problems, I'd go visit her. But my brothers are different. The initiative has to come from us. We have to invite them before they'll come. They love our parents but they have their own lives to live.

Who do you think is better off in life, men or women?
I don't know. Everyone has something. When I was younger, all the girls said boys had it better. But they have their own responsibilities. They have to support their families ... well, maybe they don't. Women are now equal, but usually men are still considered the protectors of the family and women are the ones who nurture and raise the children. A woman is a woman. She is a gentle creature. She should be tender, watchful, and always there for her children.

I still believe in my heart that I will have true love, get married, have a baby and be very happy.

I know two families that are happy ones. One was a classmate of mine who left school to have a baby. She stayed at home and said it worked wonderfully.

I also know an older couple who treat each other so wonderfully it's almost unbelievable. I'm not saying they never argue, everybody argues. But they never shout or say ugly things or obscene things to each other. And you can see by the way they look at each other that they love each other, that as long as they are here, they are here for each other. Not that they can't go out anywhere separately, but that they know about each other, that they have a common bond, and that they don't have to say it. They respect each other. They would never knowingly hurt each other.

But there are few such couples. Around me there are so many divorced couples. But I have these two examples, one older, one younger.

It really depends on the two people. It's totally in their hands. But I think there should be boundaries that people do not cross. Even if you get angry you shouldn't shout at each other. You lose something that way. Maybe for some people it works even if they shout, but my ideal is that you don't. It would make me very sad.

It would really hurt me if someone close to me shouted at me or said obscene things or said, 'you're such an idiot'. I connect such things to people who do not respect each other. It's possible not to be that way. It's the same with raising your children. Surely you can raise them without hitting them every night.

6 Petra

My interview with Petra took place in a cafe in the centre of town. She was dressed very fashionably, with plenty of makeup and perfectly groomed hair. She seemed very bright but a bit bored by the questions, and after the interview, as I waited for her to finish her drink, conversation lagged.

She did fill me in a little more on her work as a nurse in Germany. While she enjoyed the job, she said that she cannot return to it because she cannot get another work visa and would never risk working without papers. She already gets enough trouble crossing the border into Germany because of the old work visa in her passport. The last time she tried to enter Germany, the German border guards said to her, 'how do we know you aren't going back to your old job and going to stay in Germany?' She responded, 'because I would never want to live in your country again', and was pleased when they seemed shocked.

She explained that she learned both German and English from her father who was once a university professor, but was demoted from his position, because he refused to join the Communist Party. At school she studied Russian, which she now thinks is worthless. She also had some trouble in school because she refused to join any communist organizations, including those for youth and children. Her teachers would question her and push her to join along with the rest of the students, but she would simply say that she wasn't interested and leave it at that.

Finally, she told me that almost everyone who worked with her in the nursing home in Nuremberg was a foreigner. A few Germans would get a job there, work for about a day or two, and then quit because they didn't like the money or the working conditions. But, she explained, for her the money and the working conditions weren't bad, even though they weren't up to par to what local Germans would expect. This was in keeping with the general segregation of labour she noticed in Nuremberg, where most of the construction and maintenance workers she met on the street were Russian or Ukrainian. In general, she said she wasn't comfortable with Germans and found them arrogant and unfriendly.

I never wanted to study nursing. I wanted to be a rehabilitation therapist. But very few people got in to study that. And with my grades I didn't have a chance. My sister studied economics but that's too complicated for me, so I went to a nursing school.

Did you enjoy it?
The first year I didn't like it. The transition from elementary school was difficult for me. Plus we studied only theoretical subjects – things like chemistry and physics – and no practical nursing skills. I began to like the nursing school only in the second year when we started clinical practice. We also learned some nursing theory. This was completely new to me and much more interesting than the chemistry and physics we had the first year.

If you were fifteen years old now what would you choose to study?
That's difficult to say, but definitely a foreign language. I wanted to study English at school, but I wasn't allowed to. There were very few of us who were interested in it, plus we had to show that we had already studied it for two years. I had studied it, but privately, so that didn't count. But now I really miss not having studied more foreign languages.

Where did you work after you finished school?
I worked for two years in the Czech Republic in an intensive care unit. Then I went to Germany and worked for three months in a retirement home. I came back here and applied to return to Germany, but I had a lot of bureaucratic problems with that. Finally, it came through and I spent the last year and a half at the retirement home there.

How did you manage to get an invitation to work in Germany?
My friend went there first, and she talked me into it. I did not want to go at first, because I liked the first place where I worked. But then I changed my mind and decided that I would try it out. After three months in Germany, the director of the home offered me the job on a longer term basis.

How does working as a nurse here compare to working in Germany?
I can't compare it, because here I worked in an intensive care unit and there I worked a retirement home. In Germany I didn't need

any special nursing skills. It was more like helping with basic hygiene. It was very different work, but I learned skills I wouldn't have learned here, such as being more patient, thinking things through before saying them, or doing anything. And mainly I learned the German language, because when I left here I'd had about ten lessons in German, which is very little. I think the worst mistake a person can make is not to learn the language before going abroad. Then you can't even protect yourself if something should happen. You can't even talk to people – it's bad for both sides.

Would you like to return to Germany?
I'd like to because I can make much more money there. But the Czech government only allows us to work in Germany for a year and a half in total. They don't want to lose health care workers. I know there aren't a lot of us here, but I think it should be up to each individual if they stay or go.

So I think I'll go back to work in a hospital here and study a specialization such as anaesthesiology. It takes about a year and three-quarters to do, but if I want to work in intensive care, I have to get started on it within the next year.

What do you like the most and the least about nursing?
In intensive care I liked the fact that I was independent, that when things happened I had to react and think about what I would do before the doctor came.

What I didn't like was the pay and the working conditions. Everybody still assumes nursing is not hard work and that we sleep with doctors. I don't think people realize how difficult it is to be a nurse.

Did people have the same attitudes in Germany?
In Germany I was a foreigner. If I was German, it would've been different. But as a foreigner I had different problems, mainly with the language.

In the upcoming doctors strike, there's been talk of nurses joining in with doctors. What do you think of this?
I think if nurses don't speak up, nothing will change. Nobody is going to solve things for us. But to join in with the doctors would be stupid. I know we all work in health care, but if we joined them, the focus would be only on *their* demands. Their needs and our

needs are two different things. A nurse's job is completely different from a doctor's, so we need separate strikes.

What is your opinion of the privatization of hospitals?
In Germany I worked in a private retirement home. It's very different from a state-run clinic because of the attitudes there. In a private clinic you have greater respect for the patients and you learn to be more responsible. It's your job and as soon as you do something wrong, you're out on the pavement. You definitely have to be more responsible and to value the people around you more than you are used to.

Do you think things will improve here as hospitals privatize?
Definitely, because it's different to work in a state hospital or a private one. If I had a financial stake in a hospital, I would act differently, even with respect to the machines! I don't mean by that we regularly ruin the machines, but that if we owned them, we would treat them differently. In the state hospital we say, 'That's not ours . . .'

Do you think your education prepared you for being a nurse?
In the third year we had a month of 'hands-on', practical work, so we had an idea of what the hospitals look like. I also worked in a hospital on weekends. I think that our classical training is definitely better than that given in Germany. We get more practice.

But the advantage of schools in the West is that you start at a later age. Here we start too early. When I was eighteen and started working in intensive care, I was shocked by how many young people were dying there. This I was not prepared for. Our practice sessions were in internal care where we saw old grandmothers. But when you cannot help young people. . . . It was too soon to see that. It changed me. It took a long time to get used to.

Do you think a patient should have to pay for care if they are already paying for insurance?
That's difficult – a lot depends on a person's financial situation. In Germany there were people who couldn't afford the kind of home I worked in.

I think people who cause damage to themselves by doing things such as smoking should pay for their own care. I saw a show on German TV where there was a deaf man who had to pay for his own translator of sign language. He was very upset and said, 'Why should I have to pay for an interpreter when other people who smoke or drink aren't paying anything.' I think it's wrong for such a person who was born with a problem to have to pay for his care. But an alcoholic should have to pay so that they actually value the care they get and don't take it for granted.

Are you in a serious relationship?
I am. We plan to be married, but first I'd like to be financially secure so that our kids will be provided for. I live with my parents and don't have an apartment. Neither does my boyfriend, which is a problem.

Do you want to have children?
Yes.

What do you think is a good age to have your first child?
When I'm about twenty-five or twenty-six. I don't think I'm grown up enough now. I feel like I still have a lot of problems to work out, so it's not a good time now.

When you have children do you want to stay at home with them?
Definitely. I wouldn't put them into day care. Preschool is fine. They learn about being in a collective. But day care is too early. Maybe it's all right for two or three hours a day, but definitely not the whole day.

But I can't imagine how I could continue working at the hospital with all the shifts. I definitely would have to find a new job. I would need to change my profession, but I would have to adjust by, for example, working part-time.

Who in your opinion should take care of the household and the children?
Both people. Definitely not the woman alone. I think it should be shared. Not in half because some work is better for men to do, such as grocery shopping. And there's nothing wrong with a woman doing what is considered women's work.

When I was in Germany I saw a lot of men doing the shopping. They drive to the store, drive home, and don't make a fuss. Here you see women walking home from the store with ten shopping bags in one hand, a child in the other. It's a question of lifestyle. Not as many people have cars here. We don't have supermarkets

like in Germany . . . but a lot depends on how the two people decide it should be.

In your family who did most of the shopping or cooking?
My mother. And then us when we got bigger. I'm not saying my
father does nothing. Occasionally he shops. But about eighty per
cent of it is done by my mother.

**When you get married do you want your husband to do some of
the housework?**
I hope that he will help out. I think we have a different relationship than my parents have. I think our household will be different.

What do you think it means to be a good mother?
I think it's not as much a question of time but a question of talking to your children, and being interested in their problems. I don't
think that's customary here. People are more likely to say, 'Go
read it in a book.' We never had any kind of sexual education.
Today it's different. You can read about it in a magazine. Today
children are growing up in a different environment than we did.
Now children have more contact with such issues than we ever had.

And to be a good father?
That's the same. Exactly the same.

**Do you think a woman should work if the family could live off
her husband's income?**
That depends on the woman. It depends on how interested she is
in staying at home. It really would not suit me. I need contact with
people. I didn't like it when I was between jobs and spent three
months at home. But of course, I was young and didn't have children to take care of. But still, I don't think it would suit me.

What is your opinion on abortion?
I'm not against it, but I think it is a question of sexual education.
A lot of young girls depend on their partners to provide protec-
tion. They don't protect themselves, get pregnant, and have an
abortion.
   It's completely different if she's raped, or the child has birth defects.
I have nothing against that. But I'm against abortions if it's just
because the woman is sixteen and didn't use birth control.

Do you think there is enough information on contraceptives?
Now there is more, but still not enough. When I was fifteen there
was no problem in going to the doctor for contraceptives. But who
at that age would go to a gynaecologist? We had no sexual education in elementary school nor in high school. Or maybe once, in
grade 8 some doctor came in, but it wasn't anything. In fact, it was
quite comical. . . . It's completely different if the subject is treated
openly and discussed with the child from a young age, both at home,
with parents, and at school.

When did things start to be more open here?
After the revolution, magazines for young people started coming
out. It was discussed at school. Problems that 'didn't exist' here
before – that could not be discussed – such as drugs, are now being openly talked about.

**To what extent have you changed your ideas or plans following
the Velvet Revolution?**
A lot, especially during this last year and a half that I was abroad.
I have learned a lot. I have become more mature rather than simply older. I've clarified my opinions and realized my weaknesses.

Do you think you have more opportunities in life now?
Definitely. Before the revolution I couldn't have gone abroad. I
couldn't watch foreign TV. Now students can even study foreign
languages at school. They can choose English or German. We didn't
have that opportunity.

How did you learn German?
My father taught me at home. He taught me English too. He used
to be a professor, but then he was demoted.

Would you say you are content with your life?
I am.

What do you hope for in the future?
To stay with my partner. To buy an apartment, but that's financially impossible. To have a good job and find a good group of
people to work with.

7 Kamila

The interview took place at the Velryba kavárna, a – usually – quiet, low-key restaurant, coffee-house and bar that is frequented mainly by young Czechs and expatriates. But on the Monday evening that Kamila and I met, the coffee-house was packed and the crowd was a bit rowdy. In the middle of our interview, a fight broke out. It was a 'fight' in the classic sense, complete with blood, a man lying unconscious on the floor (who soon rose and started swinging his fists in the air again), a broken chair, and the bartender vainly trying calm things down. I was frightened and, after the more aggressive of the two fighters had stomped out of the coffee-shop, slamming the door behind him, I suggested to Kamila that we leave. But she was completely calm, and said she didn't think there was any need to go. Since I'd been detecting some tension around the fact that she works for the police – it was almost as if she expected me to dislike her for this – I chose this moment to joke that 'now we can see why you are the cop and I'm not'. She seemed pleased and laughed. We had just resumed the interview, when one of the fighters returned to the coffee-shop, banging the door behind him. He went up to the other man who had been in the fight, and grabbed him by the head. Again I suggested that we leave, but Kamila shook her head and watched the two men struggle. Finally, the bartender quietened them down, and the more aggressive of the two fighters left, this time for good.

With all this behind us, after the 'official' interview was over, I was still feeling a bit nervous. But we did manage to talk at some length about her work in police administration. Kamila told me about the changes in police work since the revolution. The primary difference, she said, is the rise in the murder rate, and in crime in general. Most crime in the Czech Republic, she said, is linked to alcohol abuse; in this particular week only three cases crossed her desk that were not directly linked to alcohol. When I asked her about the changes in the organization of the police force after the revolution, she said that there was more of a 'shuffling around' of people, than outright dismissal. Most of the people who were removed from the force were the 'criminology experts'. This was a bad idea, she said, since they were exactly the people who knew how to deal with criminals, while the new people who replaced them came in without a clue about how to do their jobs.

Kamila was well dressed, in a long grey skirt, a bit on the conserva-tive side. She smoked a lot, talked a lot, and spoke very quickly. She seemed very sure of herself, but also on the alert, as if ready to defend herself against criticism. In particular, she seemed prepared for me to say something critical about her father's connection to the police force (which I did not).

At the end of the interview, she related an interesting anecdote about how she and her friends like to celebrate 'unpopular' holidays. Under communism, she said, they got together and celebrated all of the 'capi-talist' holidays. Now they get together to celebrate the 'communist' ones.

I was born in Havana, Cuba, where my father worked in the Czecho-slovak Embassy. He was forty-four. My mother was twenty-six. She didn't work while we were in Cuba, but before and after that she worked as a state employee in Czechoslovakia. We moved back to Prague when I was five.

Where does your mother work now?
She does administrative work with the police. My father is no longer alive.

Is your mother happy with her job?
Pretty much. She has good working conditions. A good salary and job security. You don't get fired just like that from the police, unless you mess up.

Did your father help out with the household when you were growing up?
Help out? He was very busy at work. When he wasn't teaching, he was studying. He was a university teacher. But I guess he did what he could. But mainly he was busy studying, since he was enrolled part time at two universities.

When did you decide to go to nursing school?
I was a bit naughty when I was a child. My father always told me that he'd punish me by sending me to nursing school. So I filled out the form and he signed it. Then my mother found out. We started to think about where else I could go, because I had three

Cs in grade 8. My options were to apply to an apprenticeship programme or to go to a nursing school. So nursing school seemed
like the best choice. And I enjoyed it.

And after graduation you worked as a nurse?
I worked in a hospital on the outskirts of Prague, but the conditions were bad, because of the personnel. I got married very soon,
just after graduation. And I wanted to work only part time because I lived outside of Prague and had to commute. They weren't
too accepting of that, so I changed jobs to another hospital. I worked
there until my divorce. After the divorce I had to leave because
my ex-husband created some problems there for me. He kept coming to see me at work . . . so I left. I got a job at an insurance
company, and then at the police.

**When you were fourteen, did you consider any jobs other than
nursing?**
I thought about nursing or working for the Ministry of Interior –
the police. Ever since I started thinking about jobs I wanted to
join the police.

Why?
I have it in my blood. Both of my parents worked for the government. My father taught at the police academy. First he was in the
military. Then he worked in the 1970s with the embassy in Cuba.
When he returned here, he left the military and was unemployed –
an interesting position to be under socialism! Then he joined the
police and taught philosophy at the police academy. I was always
attracted to male professions. My mother was always saying, 'Jesus
Christ! What is my child going to become.' At one point I wanted
to be a truck driver. Then a soldier.

What did your mother think of you joining the police?
It didn't bother her. She also works at the police. It's in our family. But there are families in which you can't even mention that
you work for the police.

**If you could chose any kind of job or any kind of education,
what would you chose?**
If I could, I'd go to university. But probably I'll stay at my present
job.

What is your rank?
I'm an administrative assistant. I don't have a rank. I work in the department of transportation, but I'd like to work in the criminal investigation division. I'd like to study at the police academy.

How long would it take?
The police academy would take three and a half years. You can then work as an investigator. Alternatively, you can go to a secondary school and then enrol in a postsecondary police diploma course, which takes about fifteen months. Altogether, that would take two to three years. All of the studying would be done, of course, while working.

How long were you married?
Two years.

Could you tell me why you got married?
It was for love and also a little out of stupidity. We lived together for five months. I met him before I graduated. We got married out of love. We didn't have to get married,[1] but I didn't know that until fourteen days after the wedding. Then I found out.

Were you happy with your job when you worked as a nurse?
I didn't really like my first job, that was quite depressing, but I was quite happy on the orthopaedics ward. I had to leave it in order to distance myself from my husband. He would come there quite often. There was a problem with the receptionist, because she would let anybody walk right in. I'd be working the night shift and my husband would turn up, slightly drunk. People looked at it strangely. But the pay also wasn't that good. I worked part time because I have ulcers and could not work full time.

Did you like working with patients?
Oh yes. I think I was a favourite among them. I never had any problems with them.

Have you considered returning to nursing?
Lately I've missed it. When I see 'ER' or 'Chicago Hope' on TV, it draws me. Sometimes I read something about medicine. I try to keep up, but I'm not seriously considering going back to it.

**Do you think your education adequately prepared you for the
job?**
When I look back on it, I think I was well prepared. But I could've
done with more clinical practice before I started. In the first ward
I worked, within a month after all the new nurses started, we were
working alone, without help and supervision from older nurses, which
we should have received. If somebody had found out about this,
there would've been trouble. Everything would've come down on
the head nurse, so we kept our fingers crossed for her. Usually you
work with a partner for six months and then take an exam. Only if
you pass the exam, are you allowed to work alone. But none of us
had even taken that exam. Our noses were to the grindstone but
we learned a lot. And we had to work fast.

How many patients did each nurse have under her care?
Under normal conditions, there were twenty nurses for thirty-two
patients. This was in the winter when a lot of women slipped in
their high heels on the ice. They were lying there with concussions.
    I worked the night shift until quarter to six. Everyone was sup-
posed to be washed and ready by 6 a.m., but usually there was so
much work I didn't get done until seven. When the kitchen was
closed, I even had to hand out their meals. It was a rough day.
    At school we also had a year or two of psychology. I think this
could have been expanded, because a number of the nurses and
not just the young ones, treated the patients very badly. The older
nurses, who were set in their ways, were a bad example for the
young ones. It wasn't right. And the patients then complained to
each other – 'that's the rude nurse,' they'd say. It wasn't nice.

Why do you think it was that way?
Mainly it's in the way people are, but it's also due to what you
learn, and what you don't learn at school. I mean that for the younger
nurses. The reasons are different for the older ones. A lot depends
on the way a person approaches giving care and wanting to help
people. And the kind of wards in which they start out as nurses. I
started out in the septic unit. It's a pretty dirty unit. There the
nurses are especially numb to it all. It's a good experience, because you learn a lot and see a lot. Then when you go to a normal
ward, you won't let yourself be mistreated. But you could see that
nurses there became quite distant from the patients.

What is your opinion of the current changes in the health care system?
When I see what's happening on TV, I sometimes think this can't be possible. Maybe in Russia, but here? It's all so confusing. It should all be, so to speak, blasted into thin air and rebuilt all over again.

Today I found out that my boss's daughter has an infected appendix. Her doctor advised her that she should have it removed. She's getting ready to take her high school exams and she doesn't want to have complications during her exams. So why not have it out now? However, she was refused the operation because it's not yet an acute problem. Do you know why they turned her down? Because if it's not an acute procedure, the insurance company will only cover half the cost of the operation. So you can already see how the insurance companies are harming the patient.

In the end she went to Nymburg and they did it for her there. In a small town, people know each other. But here in Prague, there are so many people in this situation. There have been lot of cases when people were denied medical care. I think the doctors should lose their diploma for this. You're not a person if you act like this. A normal person, who doesn't have any training in health care, will help a person if they see that a person needs help. Here, we are always admiring the system in the West, but what would happen to a doctor who did such a thing in America? He'd lose his diploma! We are always admiring the American way, but doing it exactly the opposite.

Do you have anything else you want to say about health care and privatization?
It's going to take a lot more than paperwork. You can't solve such a think by having someone who has never worked in health care write something up. And that's how it's being decided now, from behind a desk.

Do you have any children?
No. I'd like to. So far I've been pregnant twice but miscarried both times. I'll see what happens, what the doctor says. Even now, I still think I have time to have kids. But of course, if I got pregnant, I'd keep the baby.

What do you think it means to be a good mother?
To know how to make time for the child. To raise the child so that they can tell me any problem they might have. They can confide in their friends, but they should also be able to share their problems at home. To be a good mother means to pay attention to your child and to know how to listen to him. And not to make light of their problems, to make fun of what they say. That's a horrible mistake to make. That's as important as the things we take for granted that a child needs, such as love.

And to be a good father?
To know how to be an example of authority. But also to pay attention to the child and make time for him. Everybody is so busy around you. One person is an entrepreneur, another has two jobs, but to be a good father is to primarily make time for your family. To talk to them, not to come home and turn on the TV.

When you have children, how long do you want to stay at home with them?
However it works out. About three years, not less.

Is it different to raise a girl than to raise a boy?
It is different. A girl is different than a boy. A boy is harder work, because naturally he is more active. Even though there are girls who are as bad as two boys! But in general girls are calmer and boys are livelier. They misbehave more. You have to watch a boy. Of course during puberty you have to watch them both! But boys are harder work. They get into more trouble.

Who in your opinion should be responsible for housework?
It's the responsibility of the woman, but her husband should help. If the woman has trouble at work or is sick, then the husband has to be able to do the basic housework. He has to occasionally show some interest. The idea that it is all just a woman's responsibility seems stupid to me. Because the man can always end up having to fend for himself.

A lot depends on how you raise your children, because if a boy doesn't even learn how to wash the dishes at home, he won't do it in his own household. Wherever you look, boys are coddled by their mothers. But then what do they do if they end up living on their own?

Does your boyfriend help you with the housework?
He loves to cook. We argue about who will cook!

That's good, no?
Well, yes. But it sometimes gets on my nerves. He loves to cook and sometimes even vacuums, the kind of vacuuming where you take it right down the middle. When I need to clean up at home I kick him out, because he gets in the way. I wouldn't let him dust.

And chores like shopping . . .?
We go grocery shopping together. We both know what we want.

Do you think a woman should work if her family can live off her husband's income?
It's up to the woman. I spent two months at home, not going to work. It was horrible on the financial side and even on the psychological side. I didn't know what to do with myself. You see it when you're sick and spend two weeks at home and you're not sick enough to just be in bed all the time. So what do you do? You clean out the cupboards, and then what?

I think if the woman's at home and has a hobby, some kind of work to fill her time is good. But for a woman to slouch around at home doing nothing cannot be good.

And what if her husband said he'd stay at home with the kids and she would go to work?
That depends on them agreeing. If he wants to stay at home, then why not? It also depends on the woman's job. If she can earn more than her husband and the situation works for them, why not? Of course if there were problems, it'd be better for them to change places and for him to go to work. She would have to have a good job and her husband would have to want to stay at home.

Do you feel any pressure from your family to marry?
No. My sister just got married. She lives with my mother. I don't live with them any more. When a person lives with their partner and they don't have children, it's not necessary to marry. In such a case, it's just a piece of paper. But when you have kids, then of course you get married. It's better not only for the child's name, but in case something happens, then the child is protected.

But no, I don't feel any pressure. And I'm not considering it.

What is your opinion on abortion?
If a woman has an abortion because she doesn't really want a child this year – she wants to wait another year – then I don't agree with that. If there is no special reason, such as a family problem, a financial problem, or lack of housing, then I don't agree. She might not be able to have children later.

But if it is necessary, if there is a health problem, then I agree. I think women should think it over more before they decide whether or not to have an abortion. When you consider that there were 30 000 abortions in a year, you can't tell me that each one was necessary. That's ridiculous.

Nobody really wants to have children nowadays. Maternity benefits haven't changed to keep up with inflation. That's why the birth rate is falling.

And then they changed the retirement age. They keep raising it until nobody will even live that long. Pretty soon I bet it'll be at 80! Now it's quite high at 60. It should be the way it was before, that a woman with three kids retired earlier than a woman with only one.[2]

Should there be a law governing abortions?
If abortion is made illegal, it will still happen. It will just be illegal. The results will be worse than if it's legal. There's now a time limit here. No doctor is allowed to perform an abortion on a patient who had an abortion less than six months ago.

That's an actual law here?
It's not the law but it's the norm. Even though today there are ways around it. You can go to a different gynaecologist and not forward your records.

The only law governing abortions should be about who can and cannot perform them. But any limitation of availability is pointless. In Poland it's illegal and all the Poles just come here.

There is a law now that you have to pay for an abortion. It costs a lot of money. But the numbers of abortions haven't gone down.[3] If people are in a desperate situation and are counting out how much an abortion costs versus the cost of raising a child, they still end up borrowing the money for an abortion. If you can't afford to have a child, you simply can't afford to have a child. Having to pay for an abortion isn't going to change that!

Who do you think is better off in life, men or women?
That's a debatable issue. Men say women are better off because
men have to serve in the military. But when men are asked to
attend a birth, they don't.

We expect men to financially support their families, which is a
big responsibility. But a woman has a job, a household to run, and
children to take care of. She has to get the child ready for kindergarten, take it there because her husband doesn't have the time.
In the afternoon she has to do the shopping. I think if you are
talking about workload, it's worse for the woman. Of course, some
men have a heavy workload or work in two jobs. He has to somehow earn money. But the woman has it worse, because she has
both employment and the household.

And then all around the world, woman is looked upon as second
best, which causes her suffering. It's considered normal when you
are driving and suddenly a car gets in your way and you have to
brake, you are simply 'a woman behind the wheel'. That's an everyday occurrence.

Do you think there's a way to change things?
That will take a long time. I just gave a friend of mine a book
about the 'woman problem'. It goes from the past to the current
situation. It's an American book. Take Japan for example. It's a
very modern country, but women there are still down-trodden, following behind their husbands. So I think these changes take a long
time. It depends a lot on how you are raised, because if a small
boy hears talk at home about 'hen brains', he likes it, because it
makes him feel superior. And he carries these attitudes on.

Who wrote the book?
If only I could remember. I think it's called *Being a Woman*. I
ordered it from a book club. The author is an older woman, she's
about seventy years old. I gave the book to a friend for her birth-
day. She read her husband a few lines from it, and he kept saying
'that's not true'. He got quite angry. I told her 'What did she expect when she read it to him?' She said, 'You're right.' I said I'd
rather hide the book from my husband so he can't read it.

In terms of women's issues, how does the Czech Republic compare to America?
I think in the Czech Republic we are about average. That's compared to Europe and America, because Asia is a different story. In China women have improved their situation. That was the positive aspect of communism, which improved women's status by allowing them to work. That's also why they celebrate International Women's Day there. But here we're maintaining things on a moderate level. It's not a total catastrophe. It's tolerable.

How did communism affect women here?
Here it enabled women to go to work. They were cut loose from the home and made useful. But after the war it was necessary for women to work. I also think they raised women's status by celebrating International Women's Day, and overall by improving women's status. The number of women studying increased. They could study law, engineering. Before there wasn't a lot of women in those areas. Becoming a school teacher, that was possible. There are films from the First Republic (1918–39) where they don't mention that a woman can be an engineer or a lawyer. After the war, that all changed for the better.

I don't know how it would have been if communism didn't happen. Of course, women would have still gone to work because it was necessary after the war. But, I don't think they would've received the same higher education. It became the law here that a woman is equal to a man, and that improved things. Out of all evil comes something good.

How have things changed now following the Velvet Revolution?
Women gained in some ways. Women can now start businesses and try to reach a higher status in society. There are more women in government,[4] even though there aren't a lot of them. In some ways it's better, in some worse – maybe on average it stayed the same.

What do you think are the greatest problems facing Czech women?
Entering male dominated jobs. These include work such as a personal chauffeur, with the police, or in government. I think women are held back in these areas. I think it would help if there were more male teachers so that children aren't just influenced by women, aren't just being bossed around by women. If a man was doing the same work, children's views about women might be more balanced.

How did your own life change after the Velvet Revolution?
A lot changed for me because my father died in November 1989.
I spent the day of the general strike arranging his funeral. It was
horrible. We were left three women in our family. I can't imagine
what it would be like if my father were still alive. He was very
influential. If he were still alive, he'd probably be unemployed now.
It's true that after he died, things relaxed a little. If he told me I
had to be home by nine, I had to be home by nine. I don't know if
my mother wanted to make up for this, but things loosened up
after he died.

After that I started a serious relationship, got married, and moved
to a village. I was responsible for the house we lived in. I had one
room to myself. The house was supposed to be given to us by an
elderly relative. I had to travel twenty kilometres to take care of
him. Plus I had a job. So it was a difficult time, a bit of a reality
shock. When I later got divorced and moved to Prague, I felt like
being lazy.

Otherwise I wouldn't say there were major changes after the
revolution, especially for those who stayed in the health care sector.
There were more beautiful women around, a boutique and a sex
shop made an appearance, but otherwise it stayed basically the same.

Would you say you have more opportunities?
It seems like it. Nurses used to be tied down to nursing. Now it's
different, a girl can find a different job. When I left my job at the
hospital, I realized I could do something different. But I found out
that there was still the attitude that what I studied was more important than what I knew how to do. When I said I studied nursing, the reaction was that I should be a nurse.

As nursing students we studied maths, but we didn't learn accounting or typing. We learned practically no foreign languages,
no typing and nothing about computers.

And what made an appearance immediately after the revolution:
job ads requiring such things as three years of experience in adver-
tising! They want three years of experience just after the revolution! I laughed – how can they require three years of experience in
a field that didn't exist here before and then want it straight away
after the revolution?

Now I think things are better because nobody cares about your
diploma. What's important is that you can do what you say you
can do. I think it's a good thing that a person can do what he/she
wants.

NOTES

1. Subsequent reference to a miscarriage, mentioned later on in the interview, throws some doubt on the assertion that pregnancy was not one of the reason for the marriage.
2. Under communism, all women were eligible to retire at fifty-seven. Women with one child could retire at fifty-six, women with two children at fifty-five, women with three children and fifty-four, and women with four and more children at fifty-three. However, most women continued working past the retirement age, because pensions were so low – only half of regular earnings. The postcommunist attempts to increase the retirement age to Western European levels has met fierce resistance from trade unions, and the population at large.
3. Kamila is wrong on this point. As indicated in Chapter 2, the number of abortions has declined substantially since 1989. The decline is generally attributed to increased reliance on contraception. However, Kamila's views on the cost of raising children, and on the decline in the birth rate, are quite accurate.
4. Kamila is wrong on this point. At the time of the interview (February 1996), there have been **no** women at all in the Czech government. Moreover, Bohumíra Kopečná, the chief public prosecutor of the Czech Republic and the *only* woman to hold a top state office, stated in an interview in 1995 that leading positions in society should be occupied by men.

8 Milena

Normally when I meet an interviewee, we spot each other right away. But when I was waiting for Milena in the metro, she walked up to me and I assumed she was someone asking for directions or for change for the ticket machines. Her demeanor, the way she carried herself, her clothes, all made her appear much more mature than a woman in her twenties. Mature, but vibrant, and very lively. She has a very relaxed and fun-loving spirit about her, even when she is talking about very difficult subjects.

Milena is also very curious. Once the tape recorder was turned off, she asked many questions, primarily about the health care and educational systems in the US and Canada. She wanted to know what happens in the US if some one without insurance is hit by a car, then who pays for their health care? What if someone without insurance is schizophrenic and needs therapy, are they able to get it? Or what if someone is going through a divorce and needs therapy, can they get it for free?

We talked for a long time about psychotherapy in the US and she expressed surprise over how psychological services are organized. She thought it was ridiculous that most therapy appointments are by the hour. At the clinic where she works, clients call up, come in and can stay up to two weeks if they need it. She was also surprised that many of the crisis hotlines in the US are not necessarily connected to therapy centers where the caller can come in and continue talking to the person they just talked to on the phone.

Her interest in the US and Canada stem from her earlier 'dream' of working as a nurse in Canada. In 1988, before the Revolution, she applied to be a nurse on a Native reservation in British Columbia. She had completed all the necessary paper work, but gave up when she tried to fulfil some of the other requirements such as learning English and being able to ride a horse.

Before we parted, Milena said there was a final question she 'had to ask me': what is the state of women's emancipation in the West? She explained that one of the clinics where she had once worked was bought out by an American company which sent them American training materials, including material on sexual harassment. She told me that she and her co-workers had laughed about how 'prudish' and 'uptight'

Americans are on these issues. She'd even heard that American women get upset if men open doors for them, an idea that she thought was ridiculous. She was very curious if this is what I think 'feminism' is all about.

My mother worked as a lab technican when I was born. I think she was content with her job, but only to some extent. She has certain moods – emotional problems – so she can never be completely content. But there was no other job that made her happier. When she was younger she wanted to be a teacher and study education. But she didn't want to study Marxism or Leninism, so she gave up that idea. Maybe it was her dream that never got fulfilled . . . but I think she liked being a lab technican.

Do you think she ever desired to stay at home?
That would have been difficult both financially and emotionally for her.

Does your father help out at home?
Yes. He washes dishes, goes shopping, sometimes even vacuums. When I was young he spent a lot of time with me. More so when he worked at the Ministry of Heavy Industry than he does now as a businessman. He spent eight hours a day at work, once or twice a month went on a business trip, and the rest of the time he was at home with his family. Sometimes I felt quite uncomfortable, that I was locked into a family. They didn't want to let me go out. I didn't have contact with other kids. That was a problem.

And now you live . . .?
On my own. Since I was nineteen. I have my own apartment.

When you were younger, did you have any plans or ideas about what you wanted from your life?
I wanted to be independent of my parents. That was very important to me. Otherwise I imagined I'd be a nurse in the operating room. And that I'd have a family and kids.

How old were you when you decided you wanted to be a nurse?
It'll sound funny but I knew from the age of three. I don't know if it came to me from a past life or if I was born with it, but it was my great dream. And perhaps that vision helped me through my growing up. But I was really drawn to it – I played that I was nurse, I read about it. I attended first aid courses already in grade one, that early.

Do you have any plans for your future now?
I'd like to have a family and kids. I'd like to continue studying psychotherapy. I'd like to work in the area of spiritual transformation. I'm doing that now, working for a female healer who does that. I feel that I let myself be led by an inner voice that knows which way my path goes. Now I feel like there are certain things I should focus on here. In the future, I'd like to travel, but not now.

Tell me more about the work you do now.
I work at a psychotherapy centre. I was accepted to work there even though I haven't finished college – I'm still studying at the philosophy faculty. But I was hired as a nurse, even though I really do psychotherapy.

What's the best part of the job?
The part I like best is the overall workplace atmosphere. My co-workers there are so open, so full of love. It's an atmosphere that encourages personal and professional development. Working with clients, I discover that there are many things that I struggled with within myself that I can now share with others. It's a great feeling of recognition and self-fulfilment. So even when I'm helping a client or solving a conflict situation, I feel that I am benefiting from my job. I feel that it is a place where I belong.

What is the most difficult part of working there?
Sometimes working there, going to school, and doing my own spiritual work is too much. I internalize a lot of things, so I'm often ill or have a fever or something.

But in relation to the work situation, I'd say that the most difficult thing is again the intense relationships. To the extent that these people help me open up, they are also very complicated people. At times the relationships are so intense that it becomes a negative thing.

How many people work there?
Twenty-five. Plus there are about forty other people working the crisis line.

How much money do you make?
Abot 2000–4000 crowns a month, for working part-time [approximately US$75–150].

Is this your total income?
My parents occasionally give me money. They pay for my apartment and sometimes give me money for clothes. Not because I couldn't live off my income, but because I couldn't pay for school. Two-thirds of my income goes to pay for my professional training. It's a big problem in psychotherapy. My colleagues pay about 35 000 crowns a year for training, and they don't even make that much! So often they have other businesses or work on the side. They invest in their training, become certified, and then have to work for a very small salary, so they never get their money back.

What did you think of the work you did as a nurse before you got into psychotherapy?
Anaesthesiology work in the operating room, that was interesting. The work demanded a lot of time and energy. I was very tired. I also felt that I couldn't do the work. I did not feel that I found myself in it. I felt that especially at the anaesthesiology unit, when nursing graduates start working there right after finishing school, they don't have the necessary training, and aren't ready for all that's involved. This makes it easier for them to be manipulated and abused by the other nurses. This was something which was quite unpleasant for me. I had a lot of conflicts with the authorities there. It was always sorted out in the end, but the others just accepted it, and took it as given that they are manipulated and taken advantage of. The problem is that they are new and don't know what they should be doing.

I think it would be good if training were extended by a year or so for some of the specialties. The workplaces would also benefit. In our unit there were forty nurses, and twenty of them left and started every year. Yet it took almost a year to learn what the work entailed. It is really that complex and demanding, for example for heart transplants. Many people did not stay even for the duration of the probationary period, because of those bad interpersonal relations.

Do you think the training nurses receive should be on a higher level?
Yes, especially for nurse specialists. Baccalaureate studies would be also good, so that nurses could not be manipulated so easily. I think it'd be good if nurses were older. Then they would be more sure of their interest in the work, and they could assert themselves better on the job. To some extent they could even learn that at school. I think the reason why the majority of nurses quit is not because of finances, but because they can't handle the interpersonal relations.

Would you like nursing to be more open to men?
Yes. The same way women want emancipation, for example to join the government, why can't men be nurses? A lot of men would be good at it. If it were better paid, then they would want to do it. I met men in my current place of work who worked as nurses, actually as specialists in psychotherapy. They are so keen on the work that they forget about the bad finances, but the family really suffers.

Do you think patients would benefit from having male nurses around?
Yes, but it depends on the ward. I think male nurses really belong in psychotherapy and psychiatry wards, and in the operating room. But I don't know about the regular wards, whether patients would want to be washed or handed a bed pan by a man.

What is your opinion of the current transformation in the health care system?
A very negative one. I think it's to the disadvantage of the patient. I don't like our system of medical insurance. A lot of people, even those with college education, have to pay for so many things now, that they can easily reach poverty level. It's been said that if someone doesn't have much money, they'll get government assistance. But, the poverty line is so low that it doesn't allow you a decent life, especially if you're working as a surgeon and trying to live off salary at the social minimum.

Another problem is that we have clients who have no insurance, or whose insurance companies don't pay us. So we see them for free. It's a problem because some doctors are beginning to turn away such people even if they need care. It worsens relations between doctors and patients.

And finally, the insurance companies choose only certain doctors to do business with. They don't like to work with doctors who work privately part-time, but are still allied with state hospitals. So it's not like you can go to any doctor. There's still going to be a line outside the doctor's door – what the market was supposed to solve, it will re-create. The patients wouldn't gain anything.

Are you in a serious relationship?
No, not right now. I have a relationship with someone . . . it looks like we'll start going out, but I couldn't call it a serious relationship yet.

Do you want to have kids?
Yes, two.

What do you think is a good age to have them?
Twenty-five, twenty-six, or twenty-four.

What do you think are the main advantages and disadvantages of not having children?
The main disadvantage is that it's against nature, it takes away from your spiritual development. Children help us grow, mature, and rediscover life. They expand the boundaries of who we are. I think it's an important think for a woman. Even if you are successful at work or artistically, it doesn't make up for it.

What do you think it means to be a good mother?
It's about your ability to love the child and at the same time accept its individuality. To respect him and to help him develop. To give him a lot and yet to be able to give him up. To bring the world to him. And at the same time to be yourself and stay yourself.

And a good father?
It's similar except he has to watch out for the financial security of the family.

Who, in your opinion, should be responsible for the housework?
Both of them.

Split down the middle?
Theoretically, yes. But the woman's role is such that the woman is bound to do more. Or that she congratulates him when he does it.

So it probably can't be completely equal. Maybe the woman wouldn't feel like a woman if it was split in half. But definitely he should help out.

He should help out with the shopping, cleaning, cooking . . .?
I mean more like fixing things in the house. Of course sometimes he should go shopping or wash the dishes. He should fill in the gaps.

Do you think a woman should work even if her family can live off her husband's income?
It depends on her, if she wants to or not. But I think it's good for both her own development and for her family that she's not always exhausted, that she brings something new, that she has something to give. A mother who works on herself, who keeps growing, is probably the best thing for a child because the child benefits from that. The child learns from both what the mother tells him, and from the whole atmosphere the mother creates with her spiritual values.

Do you feel any pressure from your relatives or from society in general to get married and have children?
Yes, from my parents. And even a little from society. My parents are very dependent on me, especially my mother. They want a grandchild. I'd like to have a child, but only when I feel that it's right. I don't want to grab a man and have a family at any cost.

What is your opinion of abortion?
I'm against abortion even though I have very open views on sexuality. I'm against abortion because the child really does feel it. I saw a film that showed how the child really feels the pain. Its heart beat speeds up and it tries to move away from the equipment that's inserted into the woman to tear him apart. I think that spiritually it is the killing of a person. I also think it comes back to the person. I've talked to people who know about this and they said that three or four years after an abortion horrible things were happening to them. Nothing in their life worked. It's as if you put out negative energy into the world – it comes back to haunt you. I know that I would find it very difficult to make a decision about an abortion if I really didn't want the child – if I were raped or something. I also think that in general it would be hard for me to have

a child without a husband. It's important for me to have a man in my life sexually and in other ways. I know it would be very difficult, but I don't think I would have an abortion.

To what extent did your plans for your life change following the Velvet Revolution?
Not at all. My plans changed but that was because I grew up, not because there was a revolution. Nothing changed. Just that I couldn't have had this job if the revolution hadn't occurred.

Do you have more opportunities now following the Revolution?
Definitely. There are now many opportunities in all sorts of things. I could decide to travel. I can get a job I enjoy. I can study. It's up to me what my limits are.

What would you like from the future?
As a wish? Love.

9 Katka

Katka and I met in her apartment on the outskirts of Prague. It was small and simply furnished. We spoke in the living room. From the beginning, Katka seemed quite defensive and almost critical. Early on in the interview she skilfully pointed out the imbalance between us by asking me back the very same question I asked her. Once the tape recorder was turned off, she asked me how come I don't wear make-up and why is my hair pulled back? She said I didn't look like I was twenty-four, but like I was eighteen. She told me that her husband was worried when she told him she agreed to an interview with a stranger so she called up the school to find out about me, but I didn't look the way her principal described me. Next she asked, 'How many children do you want to have?' And 'When?' I almost wanted to hand her the questions and run through the interview a second time; she seemed so keen on finding out the details of my life. Instead I just answered her questions as fully as I could.

She was also very curious about American culture and wanted to know if I prefer to watch Beverly Hills 90210, Dallas, Dynasty, *or* Baywatch. *'Is life in America really like these shows?' she asked. She complained that previously everything on TV was Russian, and now Czechs are 'under the Americans', and every show on TV is American. Her husband, she said, watches the women on* Baywatch *and comments that Katka's breasts are too small and that he prefers the figures of American actresses. I told her that life in America isn't really like life on TV, and spoke about various social problems in the US such as health care, poverty, crime, etc. I also told her that I would bet that most of the actresses she sees have had breasts enlargements. This seemed to please her very much.*

My mother worked in a printshop. She managed to take care of us like any other mother. Everything was very quick. In the morning she was off to work. In the evening back home to cook, shop, and take care of us but I think she had enough time for us. She did what she could.

Do you think she would have rather stayed at home with you?
Absolutely. She would have been happier. She wouldn't have had
to get up early in the morning. She had to get up at five or five-
thirty in the morning to go to work.

Where did your father work?
He was an electrician. Now he's unemployed. He's fifty-five and
they fired him.

Did he help out with the housework?
Now he does. Now he's the housewife.

And when he worked?
He did odd things, washing the dishes and such. Nothing major,
but he did what he could.

Did he spend time with you when you were young?
Yes, when he came home from work. He always spent the evenings at home. Or on the weekends we'd all go visit a castle. He
loved to travel. During the holidays he spent a lot of time with us.
He'd take us every summer to the seaside in Yugoslavia. It was
good.

When did you decide to go to nursing school?
In the 8th grade, when I was fourteen. But to say I decided ... to
tell the truth, I didn't really care.

Did you think about any other professions?
I took the entrance exams for the academic high school, I wanted
to be a lawyer. But I wasn't good at math and there were kids who
were a lot smarter than me, so they accepted someone else. For
nursing school you didn't have to know much math.

Why didn't you consider something else?
I don't know. . . . And you? What are you going to do when you
finish studying?

I hope to get a PhD and teach.
That's good. Interesting.

Do you remember when you were fifteen years old, what you thought you'd be doing now?
I don't know if I had any ideas what I would be doing. Probably not.
   At school I imagined everything completely differently. For all of us it was a big shock when we had our first clinical practice. They stuck us in internal care and gave us the worst jobs there were – the patients confined to bed. We lost all our illusions about nursing already then. My sister, she's in her second year of nursing school and she still hasn't had any practical experience. But it's different now; she can leave school and work with infants. I didn't have that option in my training.

When did you get married?
I met my husband when I was seventeen. At eighteen I wanted to get married. Luckily he was sensible, so we waited until I was twenty-one. I always imagined I'd have a family with two kids – a boy and a girl. We have the boy, I hope we will succeed with a girl.

What does your husband do?
He's an automechanic. But right now he works in health care – he drives an ambulance. But we didn't meet in a hospital. He was still doing his military service at that time. His mother was a patient in my ward and we met through her.

If you could choose any kind of job, what would you choose?
Being a housewife. I like it and I'm very happy. If I had to work, maybe I'd like to work in a flower shop, sell flowers, ceramics, or pictures, or in a boutique. If I could choose again, I wouldn't study nursing.

Why not?
I don't know. I don't consider it my calling. I never had to deal with anyone dying. I don't know what I'd do. I can't imagine how to handle it if I had to resuscitate someone.
   Sometimes I watch *ER* on TV and I can't imagine what I'd do in such situations. I think I wouldn't be able to deal with it, because I'm really sensitive to such things.

Do you ever consider returning to nursing?
Oh yes. I don't know how to do anything else. Right now, maternity leave lasts four years. If we have another child, I can stay

home another four years. So maybe, I'd return in eight years. I know, but to send a two-year-old child to kindergarten. . . . I think it's best for the kids when someone's at home with them.

Why do you prefer to be at home rather than at work?
I can set my own schedule. However I make it, so it is. I have a little routine. In the morning I get up when the alarm rings. I feed my son and turn on the TV. I don't watch TV but just so it's on. Then I play with my son and put him down for a nap at 11:00 a.m. Then lunch and afterwards a walk. I come home and my husband is there. Then we either go out together or stay in, depending on the weather. So it all depends on us. Both in the dental and the dermatology clinics I had to listen to someone else. I don't like listening to someone else.

Are you interested in the changes occurring in the health care system?
To tell the truth, all I know is that there will be a doctors' strike. At the time the evening news is on at 7:30 p.m., I have a lot of work – bathing and feeding my son. Then the news is on again at 9:30, but I'm already asleep. I don't read the newspapers. But I'm embarrassed how little I know. When I go visit my old dental clinic, the doctor I worked for tells me about this and that and I nod my head as if I know what she's talking about. I don't buy newspapers, so I don't really know very much about what is going on.

Do you have any opinion on the privatization of the health care system?
I don't know. The dental office I worked for was privately owned. On the one had it is good that the doctor can buy all kinds of new machines and is more interested in the patients. On the other hand, the nurse does nothing more than a maid's job. The doctor says: 'I pay you, so work.' That's the way it was in my office. I don't know how it is elsewhere. The doctor's attitude was such that if we didn't like it, we were free to leave. I couldn't really say anything there. But in a state hospital, one should be able to have an input. Doctors wouldn't fire anyone. But I guess it's good in some ways. They probably know what they're doing. I don't know, I'm just a housewife.

How old were you when you got pregnant?
Twenty-one, almost twenty-two

Do you have any memories of giving birth?
I was in pain for fifteen hours. It was very long. I didn't know what to do. I couldn't have had him on my own. A day after the birth I was saying I didn't want another child. But about eight days after the birth I was saying a second child would be a good thing.

Recently a friend visited me whose due date was yesterday. I don't know if she actually gave birth. She let me feel her baby kicking. I thought it wouldn't be too bad . . . but Johnny is still too small, not yet.

What is the best and worst part of being a mother?
The best? That it's nice. The worst is getting up at night – I could shoot him. I liked breast feeding. I did it for seven months. I liked how he would snuggle up to me. He doesn't wake up at night too much now. But when he was waking up five times a night, and just as I was falling asleep he decided to cry, it was horrible.

What does it mean to be a good mother?
Probably it means sacrificing yourself. Everyone is different and gives it something else. Every child is also different and wants something else.

For you, personally, what does it mean?
To be with him, play with him, raise him, teach him. He's now nine months old. The most important things for him are to eat, drink, keep dry, cuddle, and play. We'll see what comes next.

And to be a good father?
To be kind. To have authority.

How did your life change following the birth of your son?
We had to adjust. We can't go out all night. But I think it's changed for the better. We needed something. We were together already four years, so we needed something new, a change. Both of us are very happy to have him. When we were redecorating our apartment and he was at my parents' during the day, we were both looking forward to when they brought him back in the evenings.

How many hours a day does your housework take up?
All my time. I am always coming up with something. I enjoy it.
I am happy.

Who in your opinion should be responsible for the housework?
I'll tell you first how we do it, then I'll tell you my opinion. With
us, I of course take care of the household, that's because I am at
home.

But I think my husband could occasionally dry the dishes and
vacuum, which he doesn't do. Maybe once a week he dries the
dishes. I have to praise him for it, but he could do more. But it is
still better than if he spent his nights in the pub or somewhere
else. I can't complain. He's kind.

Does he spend a lot of time with his son?
He does. He has the advantage of coming home early. Johnny sees
him all the time. And he is very happy to see him. He just hears
his father's keys in the door and he's happy that his dad is coming
home. We have a very harmonious family.

At what age do you think it's good to have your first child?
At twenty-two. I don't agree with what some women say: 'first career, then a family'. I think that after the age of thirty you are too
old to have your first child. Girls get married and have children
earlier here than they do in the US. But I think that at thirty, one
is too anxious. I see how visitors react to Johnny when he climbs
on something – 'Watch out!' they cry. I take things quite differently. I know nothing will happen to him. If he falls down, then he
knows not to do it next time. Another point is – when will an older
woman have her second child? If she has it at thirty-two, then even
from a medical point of view I don't think it is a good thing. And
then can you imagine when the child is ten and she is forty-two?
She could get cancer and never get to raise him! For all these
reasons I think around twenty is the best age.

What is your opinion on abortion?
If the girl is sixteen, why not? If she's thirty-five why not? If she
has three kids and can't afford another, why not? But there are a
lot of ways to prevent it. If it's necessary, then fine. But if I was
twenty-five and didn't have any children, I'd keep it. Even if I got
pregnant now when Johnny's only nine months old. I'd keep it.

Should there be laws governing abortion?
It's a personal decision. Everyone has her own life and a right to decide if she wants a child or not. But of course, they should have to pay for the abortion. I agree with that.

Should a woman work if the family can live off her husband's income?
No, she should devote herself to her children and household. That's good even for her husband.

There are of course some women who'd miss work, who'd be bored at home. They need to be around people. But if you want to be at home and you have the opportunity, why not?

What if your husband said he would stay home with your children and you could go to work?
That's fine. My husband would make a good mother. But I think it's decided by nature that the mother belongs with the children. She is the one who should be with them. But if you look at it from the economic standpoint, if her husband is earning a lot of money, she should stay with the baby as long as she is breastfeeding. But if she is earning more than him, he should stay at home. But they should arrange things so that she can come home and see the child. She shouldn't leave at six in the morning and come home at eleven at night. The child should know it has a mom and a dad.

How would you classify yourselves financially?
We don't have much. My husband works in health care, and I'm on maternity benefits. With the cost of living today, it's not much.

To what extent did you change your ideas or plans following the Velvet Revolution?
I was sixteen when the Revolution occurred. All I understood was that a lot of people were standing on Wenceslas Square clinking their keys in the air. All that's changed for me is that they've changed the people in power and the price of bread has gone up.

Do you have more opportunities now?
What is it worth to me that the borders are open and I could go to America, if I don't have money? People say, if you don't have it, earn it. But what good is that if my father just got fired? How is he going to find work at fifty-five? He spent the last two months at

home. Nobody wants to hire someone who's fifty-five. This is the downside.

So you haven't benefited at all?
No. And there are a lot of people like us and they are silent. Nobody of course wants totalitarianism back. Maybe it's not possible to do it any differently, but we imagined it somewhat differently. You Americans probably can't understand this, having lived only under one regime. When I watch 'Beverly Hills' and 'Melrose Place' and see the kinds of worries they have! They drive to school in a fancy car and worry whether they should go out to a disco or someplace else that night! It's a little different here. I have trouble borrowing my dad's car. We live a little differently.

10 Olina

Olina and I spoke for over three hours, but the time flowed so smoothly that it seemed much shorter, and I was surprised when the cafe we met in cut us off by closing up for the night. She seemed to really enjoy the interview, and told me that she delights in spending an evening out of the house, talking about something other than her domestic duties.

Olina is remarkably direct and her first question once the tape recorder was turned off was if my answers to the questions would be the same as hers. She then went on to ask me numerous questions about my thoughts on marriage, my plans to have children, and how I hope to juggle motherhood with a career.

She was very curious about the general differences in lifestyles in the US and in the Czech Republic. We talked at length about health care and the problems individuals in the US tend to encounter due to lack of insurance coverage. She also wanted to know how the housing shortage in Prague compares to housing in the US. In addition to describing her own housing woes (many of which are covered in the transcript below), she related the story of a friend of hers who is married and has two kids, but is unable to find a reasonably priced apartment and still lives with her parents. Her only hope is to inherit an apartment from her grandmother and so 'sadly but understandably' as Olina put it, she is waiting for her grandmother to die.

Olina expressed a great deal of curiosity about the dangers of life in the US, such as the high crime rate and the availability of guns. She also revealed that she was initially afraid to meet me, and had called the school principal (from whom I had obtained her name and phone number) to check out my references. When I asked what exactly she was afraid of, she said I could have been a crazy person who would 'drag her into the bushes'. I was surprised, and wondered whether she would have met me at all had I been a man.

My mother worked in a poultry-processing plant when I was young. She worked in the mayonnaise and egg section. Later she worked for a warehouse. She just got laid off from there. She had only six months left before retirement, but now she has to leave at the end of the month. But it's no longer the same company she started working for. In the last four years, it's changed hands three times.

Is it because of the changes taking place here that she lost her job?
Yes.

Where did your father work?
He worked at an office supply company. Because of personnel changes, he also got laid off. He started working as a driver but quit that to start a private company with several colleagues. He is a driver again, but this time as a co-owner.

Was your mother happy in her job?
When I was born, I don't think she was happy. She was working there because of the government. Originally, before I was born, she was a seamstress. She reached the position of an inspector, which was an improvement from working on the sewing machine. Then came the changes in 1968 and she was demoted to the shop floor.

Why did that happen?
I was never told why, but apparently she left the Communist Party in 1968 [after the Soviet invasion] as did a lot of people. This was the consequence.

Do you think she ever wanted to be a housewife?
I don't think so. She never had any predisposition towards house-work, like continuously tidying up, or being fulfilled at home. She always went out to work.

How did she manage to combine her work with raising her children?
She managed because of my grandmother who lived with us. The person I remember the most from my childhood is my grandmother. She picked me and my sister up from school and spent a lot of time with us. Whatever my mother couldn't manage, grandma did.

Did your father help out with the housework?
Very little. He was the type of father who came home from work, lay down and read the paper. He never cooked. I saw him doing the dishes about once a year. At most, he vacuumed.

So all the housework was done by your mother or grandmother?
It was done primarily by grandma, because she was home all day.
She would cook and clean. My mother took over on weekends.

When did you decide to go to nursing school?
I never wanted to go to nursing school. I wanted to follow in my
sister's footsteps and go to an arts school. I could draw and play
the piano. But due to my grades and the attitude of my school, I
couldn't go. Two weeks before the entrance exam, I was told that
my school would not recommend me. In those days that meant I
would not get in. I was told that the only recommendation I would
get from my elementary school would be for an apprenticeship
programme rather than for a high school. Some apprenticeship
programmes offered diplomas which were equivalent to secondary
school leaving certificates. But my mother believed that my sister
and I should have equivalent degrees so we wouldn't regret it in
the future. So even if I was never going to be a nurse, she wanted
me to go to nursing school and get a secondary school diploma.

But then I started actually to enjoy nursing school. After the
first year, I thought I'd work at the outpatient department. By the
third year I decided I wanted to get the most challenging position
I could as a hospital nurse. I really liked it.

If you were fourteen years old again, what would you study?
It depends on the situation. Nursing is not booming. I liked nursing school and I liked being a nurse but I think I'd go into something that is better paid. Perhaps I'd go into business school, but I
don't know if I'm aggressive enough.

When did you get married?
When I was twenty.

How long did you know each other?
Almost a year. We decided to get married because of our dating
experiences. We were wasting our time driving back and forth from
one apartment to another. We were always tired. We couldn't just
live together because our parents wouldn't allow it and we didn't
have an apartment. After the wedding we lived with my grandmother. So that was one of the reasons we got married. Of course,
it wasn't the only one.

Where do you live now?
During the last three years we have moved four times. I moved three times, my husband four. First he moved in with me and my grandmother. We had one room and shared a kitchen and bathroom. Then I got pregnant. My husband's parents have a two-generation apartment in a housing complex. So we moved in with them and got two rooms and our own bathroom facilities. We lasted there about half a year. It's not that we couldn't stand each other, but that we wanted to be on our own without somebody making plans for us about what we should do and then telling us if we're doing it properly. So we rented an apartment outside of Prague. It was a big apartment with an even bigger rent. We couldn't afford it and we had to move back to grandma. There was no other option. Now it looks like my parents might be able to exchange their big apartment for two smaller ones. We'd get two rooms and our own kitchen facilities. It looks quite promising. It's our only chance because we can't afford to buy an apartment ourselves.

Where does your husband work?
He co-owns a company that sells office equipment. Now they're gradually expanding to sell everything. He is working on a project that would allow people to order household goods over a computer. Customers would be supplied with a disk that lists goods such as electronics, foodstuffs, beauty products, anything from several large stores. And the goods would arrive the next day. The problem is that the majority of people prefer to go into a store and physically select what they want to buy. They also really like the advice of shop assistants. My husband's company has a lot of supporters, but also many critics.

Do many average people in the Czech Republic own a computer?
At home? They don't need to have one at home. They can order the goods from work where they most likely have a computer. Then they can just ask for them to be delivered to their home address.

How many jobs have you had since finishing nursing school?
Three. For a long time I worked in the anaesthiological ward, doing resuscitations. Then I left and worked in the same ward but at a different hospital. But I didn't like the personnel there. The interpersonal relations were very tense. I didn't like how the doctors

and nurses treated each other. It was very . . . how can I say it . . . obscene. They said vulgar things. Even if they were expressing the truth, I couldn't believe they said such things in front of patients. So for moral reasons I left. I returned to my first job.

Then I got married, and we wanted to start a family. So I left my job. I also left because I hardly ever saw my husband.

My third job was at an orthodontist's clinic. I worked there for six months and then left and was on maternity leave. I had a high-risk pregnancy, so I was home for six months. And after that I stayed home on paid maternity leave.

What did you like the most and the least about your jobs?
I liked the responsibility. The trust that everybody had in me. Doctors couldn't be with their patients all the time, but I could. So they had to believe what I told them. And they had to trust that I would do exactly what they said I should do. I also liked seeing the results of my work, seeing the patients get well. They were just a hair's breath away from death when they arrived, and within a week or a month they were fine.

I didn't like the shifts. But I had to accept that. My dream is to return to that job, but because of my son, I can't. I'm envious of my colleagues who stayed a year longer than me. If I'd stayed with them, I could've gotten training as a specialist and become a head nurse. But I left because at that time my husband and family came first.

If you could now choose to be at home, or have a job as a nurse, or any other kind of job, or to study – what would you choose?
Probably a different job where I could make enough money. Nursing isn't good for that. If I was single then it would be enough. But it's not enough to pay for a household. I'd like a job that would pay well and allow me to develop myself.

Maybe I'd choose business school and start a business. I tried something like that once. I took a beauty course on applying false nails. I was licensed and had a small nail salon in one of my grandmother's rooms. But after I got married, we lived in that room, so I had to close the salon. But I'm still licensed, so perhaps if things go well and I have some money, I'll start a small company. I'd enjoy doing that once my maternity leave is over. I might combine it with the leave to fill up the time.

Do you want to have more children?
We'd like to have at least one more, as long as we can afford to, money-wise and flat-wise. But definitely not right now. If I was pregnant now, I wouldn't want it. Maybe in two or four years.

What are the best and worst aspects of being a mother?
The best is the child. That there is a person who really loves you, who looks forward to seeing you, and to whom you mean everything. The worst . . . I don't know. I have a very well-behaved child who sleeps through the night.

What does it mean to be a good mother?
I don't know what it means, but I'll tell you what kind of a mother I'd like to be. I'd like to devote myself to my child as much as I can and help him develop in the way I think is best for him. I'd like to give him everything that I think is best for him. But then not just everything. Everything in moderation.

I read a lot of the relevant literature. I followed what the doctors advised, despite the fact that other mothers and grandmothers said to do things in such-and-such way. But I stuck to my own way. I did everything according to my conscience. I have a clear conscience that I am doing the maximum for my child.

And to be a good father?
That's half of being a mother. To play with him, to fill his time when I cannot be with him. To spend all the time available with him, as much as he can so the child knows he has a father and doesn't mistake him for an uncle. I don't know how else to say it. They should have a bond. The child should know his mother loves him and will do anything for him. But then again he shouldn't be allowed to do anything he wants to. But he should feel he is truly loved, also by his father. If that is there, then the family finances are secondary.

How did your life change following the birth of your child?
I was mentally prepared for it. I was looking forward to the baby, we wanted it. I watched how my sister handled her child, so I knew what was in store for me. I cannot say things radically changed for me.

The difference is that now I don't go to work. I'm at home. Like my mother, I'm not the domestic type, I don't find housework interesting or satisfying. I spend my day with someone who needs me all the time. He is not interested in whether I have a headache or didn't get enough sleep. He just thinks, 'I'm here now and I need my diaper changed!' But that's what is nice about it.

Originally I thought I would stay home for three or more years. Now I think the opposite. I'd go back to work right now if I could make enough money to cover my expenses and to make it worthwhile. I'd do it right now! So far I'm looking for such a job that would meet these expectations.

I feel that I've stopped growing. Or that I'm regressing. That I'm closed in. My thoughts go around in circles. I really miss hearing other people's opinions on things. I have an opinion on something, my friend has one, and my husband has another – but that's all! I discuss things with my friend. We talk about our children, housework, immediate things like that. But I miss talking about politics and things like that. And when I do find myself in a larger group of people, I realize I'm really outside on things and that I miss that kind of communication. For that reason I'd go back to work, no matter what.

Who in your opinion should take care of the housework?
Both people. Absolutely. It was different in my parents' household, but I'd like it this way. Recently most of the housework has been my responsibility. This is understandable because I'm at home a lot more than my husband. But once I start working, we should help each other out. I'm not saying he doesn't help me out now. He does as much as he can. For instance, even though I practically take it for granted, he spends time with our son when I'm cooking. Or he takes our son and together they vacuum. In the meantime, I can do something else. For example, I can do this interview because my husband is giving our son his dinner and putting him to bed. Otherwise, I couldn't be here.

How much time do you have left for your friends?
Once I went on maternity leave, I fell out of the circle of friends I used to have. Friends of mine who I used to work with have different interests now than I do. Nursing can only be done by single women, or married women without children. So those friends are gone.

I have new friends who also have children. We get together whenever we can. In the evenings, it's fine with my husband if I go out, but it also depends on my friends' husbands. I have a friend whose husband doesn't look at it the same way.

Who do you think is better off in life – women or men?
Everything has its good and bad sides. I look at it from where I'm at. Right now, I'm unhappy that I've spent the last year and half at home. But my husband has the burden of having to support us. So we each have something. But since giving birth wasn't that horrible for me, I have to say I don't think I'm badly off.

To what extent did your plans or ideas change after the Velvet Revolution?
I have the same plans; they haven't changed. I was at a stage in my life where the changes seemed automatic, normal. They didn't bother me.

Do you have more opportunities now?
Absolutely. I can start my own business. I can develop myself the way I want to. I believe in that.

On the other hand, society is harder now than before. Take for example my husband's business. Either it's going well or it's not. It prospers or goes into debt. It's based on his abilities and what he's doing.

Does your son have more opportunities?
Certainly. He can grow according to his own disposition even linguistically. He can choose where he wants to go to school. He definitely has more opportunites than we did. Now he just has to use them.

Would you say that you are satisfied with your life?
If I look back on it, I should have probably waited to have my son later, but not much later. When we were deciding whether or not to have a child, having a baby was more important than anything else. Now I would like to have stayed on at work and improved my education, had additional training as a specialist so I'd feel more valued. It bothers me that I'm at home now. I want to go back to work.

11 Alexandra

The interview took place in a small town in Moravia where Alexandra lives. She met me at the central bus stop and drove us to a local restaurant where we had coffee. Once the 'official' interview questions were completed, she suggested we have lunch. In total, we spent three hours together.

Alexandra asked a number of question about the US. She primarily wanted to know how young Americans spend their time. 'How much money do young people have to spend on themselves?' she asked. 'When they go to university, do they live in dormitories or can they live on their own? Can they afford to go out to eat or do they usually cook for themselves?'

The O.J. Simpson verdict having just been announced, she was curious about what I thought about the trial. This led to a general discussion about race and racism in the US. Like most Czechs, Alexandra expressed curiosity mixed with fear towards African-Americans. She asked if the interviewer, who is white, would cross the street when she saw a black person approaching on the sidewalk. 'That's what I do when I see a Gypsy,' she said, expressing the commonly held prejudice against Roma (Gypsies) as dangerous criminals.

Despite her comment during the interview that she is uninterested in politics, Alexandra talked at great length about political issues. She was particularly interested in questions of punishment and justice. We had a long discussion on the death penalty; she supported it, while I argued against it. Her primary justification for the death penalty was that if someone commits a crime such as murder, they deserve a punishment 'that fits the crime'. I asked about the problem of people who are put to death but later found to be innocent: 'If they went to prison for five years and were later released, they would still have their lives,' I suggested. She responded that to spend five years in prison leaves you so hurt and damaged by your experiences in prison, that your life is not worth living. 'If they kill me or send me to jail for five years, it is the same,' she said.

She also talked at great length about her political perspective on the Czech Republic. She supports the pro-reform government of Prime Minister Václav Klaus and thinks that the shift towards a capitalist economy should be occurring faster. She is upset that many of the

*communists in power were not 'punished' for the 'sins' they committed
under communism. She criticized President Václav Havel for his 1990
granting of amnesty to prisoners. Alexandra thought that this just put
more criminals out onto the street. 'Havel is too soft,' she complained.
What the Czech Republic needs, she said, is 'toughening up'.*

   *Interestingly, she herself embodied her talk of how Czechs are not
so open-hearted (especially Czech nurses). Off-tape she spoke very harshly
about people who can't find work or make their own way in life.
'People should learn how to think for themselves,' she said. 'They are
too "soft" and used to the communists giving them everything,' she
declared. She spoke very despairingly about a friend of her husband
who is now out of work. She complained that he doesn't know what
to do with himself. Given the situation where he has to find himself a
job, he is hopeless. But if he was told to sweep the same street thirty
times in a row, he would be very happy to do it. 'This is what the
communists did to people,' she declared.*

I got married when I was nineteen. My husband lived in Znojmo,
a small town in Moravia, and I lived in Prague. We met in Prague
where he was stationed for his military service. He finished his service
and was returning to Moravia. We wouldn't have been able to see
much of each other, so we got married.

   I actually only worked for eight months in Prague after I finished school. Then I moved to Znojmo, where there was no work.
I was unemployed and then I got pregnant. I had a baby and stayed
at home on maternity leave during which I sometimes worked in
my father-in-law's grocery store. In the evenings I'd put the baby
to bed and work for three hours.

When you worked as a nurse, did you enjoy it?
I enjoyed it very much. From the age of fifteen I spent my holidays
working in a hospital. But after my husband had a car accident in
Germany, I spent a lot of time with him in the hospital in Germany. Now I can compare how nurses relate to patients here and
in Germany.

   What I don't like about the hospitals here is how they relate to
patients. We still have a lot to learn. When I was eighteen and
started working in the hospital, we treated the patients – and the

nurses who are now working there still treat the patients in this way – too abruptly. We would do the work quickly, have a cigarette break, and then rush through some more work. The patient wasn't our first priority.

I had a very bad experience when we went after the accident to a famous hospital in Prague. They looked at my husband as if to say, 'What's wrong with him? He can't walk?' They had a very strange attitude towards him. When I questioned them or when I said, 'He needs to drink a lot of mineral water,' their answer was, 'We don't have any. You go and find some. We just have tea.' It was a bit of a . . . well, a bit of a shock.

Did you learn much about attitudes to patients at school?
At school we learned about how nurses should approach patients. But when you go to work, it's different. I don't know how it happens. You just fall into it. I was the type who spent a lot of time talking to the patients, waiting with them. But the others. . . .

Maybe if a whole group of young nurses, a whole graduating class, went into a brand new ward, it would be better. But instead you join a group of nurses who have been there twenty years, nurses in their forties and fifties who are worn-out, who just well, veg-out.

Do you think Czech society discriminates against disabled persons?
I've only become acquainted with this over the last year, but I think that what a person doesn't fight for, they don't get. I think there are plenty of organizations here to help out, but basically it's up to the individuals.

For my part, when I used to see a person in a wheelchair, I thought 'poor thing'. I was sorry for him. Now I am aware that so many people in wheelchairs I know are great people. They talk, converse about different things, play sports – they are just the same as us except they can't walk. Before I didn't take it that way. I felt sorry for them, but I didn't know any of them.

In any case, I think this society has a lot to improve upon. Friends have told me what it was like to be disabled during the communist regime and it was much worse. At least now things have improved and people have more opportunities.

What was it like before?
A friend of ours told me a bit about it. He played basketball and sold wheelchairs – he'd go door-to-door. He said he often almost

broke down in tears when he saw people trapped in their apartments. They couldn't go out at all if their families didn't have enough
money to buy a ramp to put over the stairs.

All these people needed was an apartment that was wheelchair
accessible, rather than being put away in an institution. When you
look at these institutions. . . . I visited a rehabilitation institution
where the patients were really suffering. There were young boys
there whose families gave up on them. They didn't want them at
home or maybe they didn't have the right facilities for them. Maybe
they felt too old to care for them. In any case the parents put
them in an institution where they now have a room 3 m by 4 m in
which they have a bed and a TV. Basically they sit there and wait
for the nurse to come by. There is a pub in the courtyard and the
young people go there, instead of exercising or doing something
for themselves. Instead they drink away their disability pension. Of
course there are exceptions, but in general the most they do is
wheel themselves outside on a sunny day which I think is horrible.

**Do you think the privatization of hospitals and of the health
care system in general will make things better or worse?**
I think things will get better once hospitals are privately owned.
But again you have to have enough personnel, because if the private hospital doesn't have enough nurses and hires anybody just to
have enough people. . . . If you instead have two unemployed nurses
for every employed nurse, then she'll think quite carefully how she's
going to behave towards patients, if she is basically going to ignore
him or if she is going to behave decently.

The problem is that in Prague there are not enough nurses. The
worst nurses are in Prague. It's horrible to say, but even when you
compare the Czech lands to Moravia, it's the worst in Prague. I
met some boys at the rehab centre in Moravia who ran away from
a rehab centre in the Czech lands. They told me about a nurse in
their old centre who went up to a disabled boy who jumped into a
pool and broke his back. The nurse laughed at him and said, 'HA!
HA! That was your last jump!' That seems unbelievably cruel to me.

After a year of this, it's really beginning to get to me. Just realizing how much it entails. . . . Say you are driving somewhere and
you want to stop for lunch. You pull over at a restaurant, but there
are stairs there. . . . Then again, I've never met people who wouldn't
help us. I say to them, 'Please could you help me lift my husband
up the stairs? I can't manage it on my own.' And they help me.

The problem is at the social service agencies. As long as no disabled people work there, they can't understand our needs. In the Czech Republic people think that an 'invalid' in a wheelchair is supposed to be poor. If he does have money, then they think, 'Aha, he must've stolen it.' They don't think that a person in a wheelchair can have a house, a happy family, and a job. If he does have this, then they don't admire him. Instead the social services agencies try to take things away from him. They say he doesn't need social services. This happened to our friend who spent nine years in a wheelchair. He's raising his daughter alone because he and his wife divorced soon after the accident. His daughter was three years old then. His mother helped out with her, but he was basically raising her on his own. He applied for various things at social security, but also got a job on the side, since he couldn't live on his tiny disability pension. He had a friend who emigrated to the US and who deals in cars that are converted for use by physically-handicapped people. He started fixing up such cars here. And because he often had parked in front of his house three or four American cars, the social services agency decided that he didn't need additional support. For example, when he applied for a subsidy to buy a car, to which he is legally entitled every two years, they said he wasn't needy enough. All because he was helping others – I think that's terrible.

Does your husband get state support?
My husband has been on disability for the last few months, so he receives some money. As his wife and care provider, I am entitled to receive a caring allowance by the state to nurse him, so I am staying at home with him.

We don't have financial problems. I can't complain about that. My husband was injured in Germany and the insurance coverage there was good enough, so that we have money. But for people who don't have another income, state support isn't enough. It's enough for food but after that you'd have to count every crown. Such worries as can I buy a pair of shoes or not? Should I buy them first for my child or for my husband? I don't have such worries, thank God.

Do you want to have more children?
I would like to but we don't know if we will be able to.

What do you think are the advantages and disadvantages of not having children?
The advantage comes from not being responsible for anyone. You can go wherever you want, whenever you want. You don't have any problems, any worries. When you have children, your life is richer. It's a wonderful thing, but you must devote yourself to them. You are held back from doing certain things, you are not so independent. First you have to make sure your child is well-cared for. You have to subordinate yourself to the child.

Does anyone help you with the housework, or do you do it on your own?
I do it all myself.

Does it take a lot of time? Do you enjoy it?
I wouldn't say I enjoy it, or that, say, cooking is my favourite thing to do. That's just the way things are; I have to make sure that there is food on the table and that the house is clean. But then again I'm not one of those tidy people who sees a bit of dust and immediately has to be rid of it. If my daughter has her toys thrown around the room, I just leave them. After all, she is just a child, so she should be able to play. However, somebody else may say: 'Well, this is really messy here.' We don't take it like that – every three days we pick it all up, so that it doesn't overflow, but otherwise we let her play.

Who in your opinion should do the housework?
I think it's up to the wife.

Why?
I don't know why.

What if the husband wanted to do it?
If he wants to then he can. I could never imagine a man taking care of my household. My husband was able to earn money and provide for us. I think it would've been too much at that time to have asked him to cook or clean. As long as he'd have wanted to take care of the housework and not have a job, then fine – I have no problem with that.

Do you think a woman should work if her family can live off her husband's income?
I think that's up to her. I think that a woman often misses her job. I know that I miss my job. Right now I am so-called taking care of my husband. He doesn't really need a specialist's care. Most of the time, I just accompany him, take out his wheelchair. . . . I help him to exercise, take him to physiotherapy, but that's about all. He is very independent.

The truth is I miss my job. I don't just want to be at home and do nothing but cook and clean and be with my husband and child. I think a woman should not work eight or twelve hours a day, but six or three. I did that after my child was born and it got my mind off my responsibilities at home. I think if a woman is only at home, she regresses. I see it in myself. I've forgotten a lot of things, because I am no longer around people, no longer talking about things. Take for example nursing. Certain things I'll never forget, like giving an injection, but if someone asked me now, I probably wouldn't know how blood circulates. That might be a bit of an exaggeration, but take drugs. I used to know all the different drugs. Now if someone told me to mix such and such a drug with another one, I wouldn't know what they're talking about.

Does you husband help you with the childcare?
Well, how would I put it. . . . When he was healthy, he would play with her, horse around with her. Now it's the same but he can't do as much with her. He can't take her for a walk or into the woods. But, he can play with her and take care of her. It's no problem for him to bathe her, dress her, or feed her.

Have you changed your plans for yourself since the Velvet Revolution?
I am not the kind of person to plan far ahead. I wanted to finish school and get a job, that's all. What will come will come. I never had any future plans.

Is there anything you are now planning or hoping from the future?
I hope that my husband will walk again. We are doing everything to make that happen. We aren't leaving that to chance.

12 Lenka

Lenka is a very relaxed, confident and eloquent woman. Unlike many of the interviewees, she gives the impression of being very 'professional' – both in her appearance and in the directness of her speech. We met at a tea house and spoke for two and a half hours, until the tea house closed. Out of all the women I interviewed, Lenka stood out for her desire to engage in new ideas and really run with them. Even though she had never been to the tea house before, she immediately began to comment on the atmosphere and how the place was set up. At the end of the interview, she said that she and her husband were thinking of opening a coffee-shop or a bed and breakfast establishment, but perhaps they should consider opening a tea house similar to this one.

Lenka has had a lot of contact with Westerners through her work in real estate. In addition to German, she speaks fluent English. She has also travelled extensively in Western Europe and has a very good idea of what life is like outside of the Czech Republic. She was, however, very curious about one aspect of the US – like many of the other women, she was very interested in the TV show 'Beverly Hills 90210'. She wanted to know if the show really reflected life in the US. I said no, and pointed out that most people aren't as wealthy as the characters on the show. She said that it's not their wealth that interests her, but their sense of morality and their reactions to life. 'Do Americans really take small things, such as your brother or sister saying something rude to you, so seriously?' she asked. She thought that the show was definitely overdramatic.

She also wanted to know if apartments are as hard to find in the US. Like most people, she thinks rents in Prague are astronomical, primarily due to the fact that foreigners are able to pay much higher rents than the average Czech. Ever the businesswoman, at the close of the interview she gave me her card and said I should call her if I ever need to move.

I was originally supposed to attend the academic high school. But then my father bought me for Christmas a book about a girl who studied nursing. It captivated me and I decided to study nursing for that reason alone. I personally now think that very few people know at fourteen what exactly they want to do as a profession.

Where did you work after you finished nursing school?
First I worked in a hospital. I worked nine months in orthopaedics which was very hard work. There were not enough nurses so we didn't have time to take the breaks we were supposed to have. And it was very hard work lifting and carrying patients, mainly old people recovering after accidents. So it was physically very demanding. And the pay was very low, very low.

When I worked at the hospital, we had thirty to forty patients to four nurses. The patients were all immobile, quite helpless. A good half of them were older people with broken necks. Their bells were always ringing. We were trying to cover the basic things, though at school we learned that in our free time we were supposed to cut the patients' nails. We didn't have any free time! Quite often patients would complain that they had already rung twice. Maybe they thought the nurse was busy drinking coffee, but we were running around taking care of other patients! From a certain perspective, nursing is thankless work, because often the patient shouts at the nurse, the doctor shouts at the nurse. And the janitor also shouts at the nurses, because there are too few janitors. I always felt that the nurse is the lightning rod of the hospital. Really, it's a difficult job.

I left because physically I couldn't handle it. Working sometimes in the morning, sometimes at night, sometimes in the afternoon. After six months of that I was like a ruin, just going to work and sleeping. I wasn't doing anything else. So after nine months I left. I originally thought I'd get a job as a nurse in a different ward or in an outpatient clinic. I enjoyed the work. I like nursing, I just don't like the working conditions. So I left.

My friend who was a chef in a restaurant got me a job there as a coat checker. So for a month I sat in the coat check. At first it was terrible, because I was used to running around in the hospital. Now I was just sitting there and every half an hour somebody walked in and handed me a coat. I felt like I had to do something! It felt completely pointless. But it had one big advantage. When I worked in the hospital, I lived only ten minutes away. In the morning I'd leave in my jeans and t-shirt and at work I'd change into my uniform. Then back into my jeans and t-shirt for the trip home. I didn't really take care of myself. But at the restaurant I had to be well dressed, made up, and with a smile on my face. And sometimes I got to speak English. So even though most of the time it was boring, physically and emotionally it was better than nursing. I got myself back together in that job.

My next job, well it wasn't really a job, but I helped out my boyfriend in a wine bar. I made a little bit of money from time to time. I was looking for a new job. I thought I'd go to work as a secretary. But I didn't have many of the required skills. They all want you to know how to type and speak a foreign language well. I spoke English very badly at that time, using only infinitives. But I got lucky and got a job at the Federation for the Disabled. The director there couldn't see very well and needed a secretary immediately. I was the only person available, so he hired me.

I was teaching myself how to type. I drew the keys on a piece of paper and filled in the letters with the help of a friend of mine who studied business. I trained on that for two days and then went for the job interview. He asked me if I could type. I said 'I can type with all ten fingers.' He looked at me and said, 'and how fast can you type?' I said, 'you know, I'm a beginner, but I type with all ten.' I just kept emphasizing that I use all ten fingers. He said, 'how long does it take you to type a page?' I didn't know what to say. I'd never typed a whole page! So, I said, 'I've never timed myself, but I type with all ten.'

That was on a Wednesday. He said to come back on Friday and the old secretary will explain the job to you, and Monday you'll begin. I nodded. On Friday when I arrived he said he was going to dictate a letter to me in English. It was hell! I sat down at the typewriter and I knew he'd say I shouldn't bother coming back to work on Monday. He started to dictate and I sat there floundering. It was horrible. Of course, after the first word he could tell that it would be awfully hard to continue. But I have to say that he was a great boss because he kept dictating. I pulled the letter out of the typewriter and it was all smeared, with parts crossed out.

He looked at it and said, 'well, your speed is horrible, and it has to be rewritten, but come back on Monday'. So he saved me. He gave me the job. At that job I learned absolutely everything; how to type; how to use a computer; all kinds of office skills. I stayed there for almost a year. After one year there was nothing left for me to learn. I wrote letters, I answered the phone. I also acted as a driver, which I enjoyed because I like to drive. At first I was afraid to drive the minibus because it's different from driving a car. But I quickly learned. It was a great job because I was only a secretary, but I went with him to government offices to handle things. Because he couldn't see well I read to him, it was interesting, but after a while it was always the same thing, over and over again.

I was then given the opportunity to work for the Academy of Sciences and I took it. After about a month, the office was reorganized and, along with another office, we became the office for foreign academics. The school was for Czechs, Romanians, Ukrainians, Bulgarians, and Poles – students from all the former communist countries. They were engineers studying for their PhDs. My job involved being a secretary for visiting foreign professors. When a professor was to arrive, he would write or phone me with a request for an apartment. I also did traditional secretarial work.

I worked there for about a year and during that time I became friends with the realtors who found apartments for us. After a year, the realtors asked me if I wanted to work for them. I knew English. I had a car. And they needed another person. So I started working in real estate and I'm still doing it today. It'll be about two years now.

I'm basically co-manager along with the other two realtors. I enjoy this job the most. I meet a lot of new people which is fun. There are sometimes days when it isn't so great, but most of the time it's fun. I've stayed at this job the longest.

Do you have a monthly salary?
You could say that. But it depends on what happens every month. I don't have a constant salary, but I can make more in this line of work that I made as an employee under bosses. It's nice to be able to determine one's own earnings. When you're trying hard, you could make quite good money. It's not like when you sit somewhere from eight to four. You could say that regardless of if it's cozy, or if you kill yourself, the rewards are the same. Here it really depends on how much you work and what you do. It suits me.

If you could choose any job or go to college, or be a housewife, what would you choose?
Maybe I'd go to school except that I've already been married for two and a half years and we're planning a family. . . . If I was single, I'd go to college. But since I'm married, I don't think I'd enjoy student life. I wouldn't be in the right frame of mind. But I wouldn't

want another job. I'm happy in the one I have. I don't really think about what I'll do in the future. Now I have this and if something else comes up, I'll think about it.

Do you want to have children?
I do.

How many?
Two or three. But most likely two. We'll see.

What do you think is a good age to have your first child?
Between twenty and thirty. I don't believe women should give birth for as long as they can. I think they should stop having children at the age of thirty, even though one can dispute it.

The most important thing is to have them when you want them. When you have a place to live, a good husband, and you say, 'It's a good time to have a baby' – that's the time. You can't say you should be twenty or thirty-five. If there is health and other conditions, there should be no rule.

What in your opinion are the advantages and disadvantages of not having children?
I don't really know, but I think that if somebody decides not to have children even if they can, they are adventurers, someone who is always on the move and who considers children secondary to that. As long as they are happy with that and won't at the age of sixty tear out their hair because everybody else around them has grandchildren and they have nothing, then why not?

Children mean worries. Only sometimes do I think having them is a normal thing. Theoretically they are somebody who will later on take care of you. But it's true that if you don't have them, you can spend all your money on yourself, on your apartment, on travelling. Both have their advantages and disadvantages.

What does it mean to be a good mother?
I haven't had a chance to try it yet. But if I look at my parents, I think my mother was a very good mother. Still is. If only because I was never afraid to come to her and say, 'Mom, this has happened' or 'Mom, what do you think I should do?' We are completely open and I can tell her everything. She very calmly gave me advice on everything. Often I was scared and she just laughed

the problem off. We had the kind of relationship friends have. But even though we dealt with each other on an equal footing, it wasn't like I put her down. If my mom said 'no' I respected that. I value her opinion and I think she is very wise.

We always got on very well. She didn't spoil me or my sister, so we both grew up very realistically minded. I really appreciate that she was not the kind of mother who tells you in front of company 'sit up straight! Lean over! Say this!' She never did that. She said such behaviour really puts the child down. It's true that afterwards she said she was very lucky that we never did anything like pick our noses at the table. So she never had much reason to remind us to behave.

I have one friend whose mother, I could say, puts her down. When we were sixteen, seventeen and went out to discos, she would say, 'Oh the two of you will end up dancing with each other again! Ha ha ha! I can already see it!' She downright lowered her self-esteem. While my mother would have said 'So girls, go out and paint the town!' I have to say I'd like to be like her one day.

What do you think it means to be a good father?
It's good when a father knows how to play with his kid. And explains things to him. I like it – and I hope my husband is like this – when a mother tells the child to do something and the child doesn't listen, and the father says, 'If you don't listen to your mother, you'll have me to deal with.' So he doesn't leave the parenting to the mother. The ideal father. . . . I don't know. It's true that my father is very kind. He loved us all. Played with us, read us bedtime stories. But he left almost all the parenting to my mother. Except when it later came to whether or not I could go away for the weekend and my mom said, 'ask your father'. Then my father had the final word. But most of the parenting was up to her. He didn't try too hard. I think a good father should have authority but should also be a friend.

When you have children, do you want to stay at home with them?
Absolutely. Definitely when they are small. I think it depends also on the situation. Perhaps after they reach the age of two, I'll have to go to work. But if not, I don't see any reason not to stay at home.

For how long?
Until they are about four and go to school.

Who in your opinion is responsible for the housework in a family?
I think the woman. It's good if the husband helps out. For example my husband really enjoys cooking. It's very nice when I come home from work and everything is simmering.

I have to say my husband really does help out. The pre-Christmas clean-up we split in half. He vacuums, washes the dishes, does a lot of things. But if he refused to do it – I think it's a woman's job.

Why?
I think it is. Men's work is to make sure the family is financially cared for. He makes sure that the broken washing machine gets fixed. Or he drives the car to the garage when it needs servicing. Otherwise the work around the house is women's work. Though you can't really say what is men's and what is women's work. There's also the issue of who likes what, and what they can do. I just said a man should take the car to be serviced, but in our family, I do the driving. My husband has a driver's licence but almost never drives. He doesn't like it and it frightens him. So it's true that he cooks and I take the car to be fixed. With us it's the opposite of how it should be! So you can't say for sure.

Do you feel any pressure from your relatives to have children?
No.

Did you feel any pressure to get married?
No. It was the opposite. Everyone was shocked when I said I was getting married because I had never considered or talked very seriously about it, and suddenly I said I was getting married. My parents were completely baffled. It's true that we only knew each other a short while, for about a year. My husband taught me English. We got together totally by chance. It's a funny story.

We met when we were sixteen. We went out once to a disco and once to a fair. He was fat and boring, horrible. So after those two dates, I said 'let's just be friends'. We never called each other again. But I kept his phone number.

When I was twenty I found out that the American Hospitality Centre had advertisements for people who gave private English lessons. Most of them were Americans. I decided I'd learn English so I went there. There was a boy there and I asked him if he knew where the ads were. He said he didn't, and told me to ask somebody up front. But then, he kindly called out to me, 'Miss! I'll teach you for free!' I went to the front and they sent me to the back again. So I went back to him and he asked me what my decision was on his offer. And then I recognized him. It was the same guy I knew at sixteen. He was thinner and I have to say he looked a lot better than when he was sixteen!

Did he recognize you too?
No. I used to have permed hair but by then I had a bob. I also wear glasses which I didn't at sixteen. So he didn't recognize me. I said to him, 'you'd really teach me?' He looked at me and said yes. So I said, 'OK, so I'll call you tonight at home.' Because I still had his phone number at home. He stared at me and said, 'how come?' I said, 'I have your phone number at home.' That sent him whirling. He said, 'Do we know each other?' I said 'of course' and then finally I told him. To this day I don't know if he was only pretending not to recognize me.

We started meeting the following week. For about four months he really only taught me English. We had our lessons in coffeehouses. Then we started dating, and then we got married. So we knew each other for a year but only really dated for six months. We got married fast. My parents were very surprised. When I was still only learning English from him, my mother asked 'What about that Paul?' And I said, 'Oh Paul!' Then we got married.

What was your reason for getting married?
I don't know. We were getting along. He came up with the idea and took it very seriously. I was always, you know ... dithering. 'I'll get married and have loads of children.' But I never took it seriously. He took it very seriously. So we married. And it's wonderful.

To what extent did you change your future plans following the Velvet Revolution?
Probably a great deal. I'm not sure how much though. Before the revolution I was seventeen and I didn't have many plans. I did not think that after I got married, I would have an apartment and get to travel abroad. It used to be the pattern that every five years you'd have a vacation in Bulgaria. Now you can travel. The standard has increased enormously.

If the revolution hadn't happened, I'd probably still be working in some hospital. I wouldn't have known what real estate is!

Do you have more opportunities now?
Absolutely. But I didn't realize that before. I think that even shortly before the revolution it was possible to travel abroad.

When I was small, I didn't realize these things. It's true that I was affected by the death of Brezhnev, because we all had to wear black. But from the perspective of someone who was a small child, it didn't affect me all that much. If I were ten years older, I would have been certainly affected. The worst off were cohorts in the 1950s when it was here very. . . . I cannot really talk about it because I know it only from films. To travel abroad required a lot of effort. My sister once spent the night in a sleeping bag in a queue in front of an embassy to get us a visa. It wasn't like it is today when you go to a travel agency for your ticket, and off you go.

My parents also told me not to mention at school that we were going abroad. Everybody would wonder, 'Why them? How is it possible?' But as a small child it didn't affect me all that much.

Otherwise I remember that we had a hidden record by Kryl. He was a singer who sang anti-Russian songs and later emigrated. It was illegal to listen to his records, much less to own them. We had borrowed some of his records from my mother's friend. I really liked the songs. I started singing them somewhere and my parents gave me a good dressing down that I couldn't do that. I wondered, as an eight-year-old, why I couldn't sing them, but I didn't care that much. If they said not to sing them, then I sang something else. It surely affected the adults more.

When we went abroad, it was a big change. When we drove over the border, all this was far away and behind us. Here it all seemed so gray.

Where did you go?
To Germany. We travelled a lot. We drove through Germany, France and Spain. My mother had a great uncle in Germany. He lived on the Czech–German border in the Sudetenlands where all the Germans and Czechs mixed together during the war. His wife was German and died during the war. After the war, he was forced to move to Germany.

We were lucky that we had a relative whom we could visit. In Germany everything was totally different. Here we had nothing.

Now it's completely different. You go to the store and there are twenty kinds of yoghurt. That didn't exist here at all. In those days we were shocked when we went to the store in Germany. There were huge freezers with everything! Here we had just one kind of yoghurt – white, with marmalade at the bottom. It sounds quite petty, but as a child that's what I noticed.

When we would return home I was looking forward to it because in Germany I couldn't talk to anyone. But when I look back on it, I realize my parents surely came back with very heavy hearts.

13 Veronika

Sometimes an interviewer and a subject develop an almost instant rapport. Other times, such an understanding takes longer to develop. And sometimes, it just doesn't happen at all. Such was my interview with Veronika. From the first minute we met, it was clear that any attempts at communication between us were going to be fraught with difficulties.

The interview was further complicated because Veronika scheduled it during her lunch hour, so we had approximately forty-five minutes to whiz through the questions, while she snacked on McDonald's french fries. Even if we'd wanted to talk informally, there was no time for it. Given all of these constraints, it is amazing that such an eloquent interview was the result.

Why did you want to be a nurse?
I always liked watching nurses on TV. I liked their caps. So when I was fourteen and had to choose a profession, I chose nursing, thinking I would one day marry a doctor. I was very young.

But later I enjoyed the work. It felt very good when you took care of someone, he got well, and then he came to you and thanked you. It might sound clichéd, but that was the best part of the job – helping people. Of course there were always people who left the hospital and never remembered you again. But a lot of people came and thanked us for improving their stay.

How long did you work as a nurse?
I worked until I got pregnant. I got married while I was still at school, around the time I graduated. It was marriage for love. Then I went to work for about a year, got pregnant, and took maternity leave. I was at home for three years. Now I work as a secretary.

Why did you stay at home with your child?
I thought that it's better to stay at home so I could see how my child grows. I didn't want to miss that. Work will always be there – it won't run away from me.

If you could still be at home, would you prefer that?
Oh no! Being at home was boring. Three years was enough. But I think that when the child is very small, it's important to be there with him. But I couldn't stand to be home for five or six years. I would return to work and do something, so that I wouldn't have to stay at home.

Does your husband help out with childcare?
I'm divorced. Actually, we've been going through the divorce for the last three years. It's not official yet. But we haven't lived together for the last two years. And no, he didn't help out very much.

Where do you live now?
I live with my parents. There are four of us – my mom, my dad, me, and my son Petr.

My parents help out in a lot of ways and I am glad that I have them. I work until four o'clock but my mother only works until three, so she picks Petr up at kindergarten. She regularly takes care of him at weekends. They often take him to the cottage when I don't come with them. So when I am with them, I have more free time because they take care of him. It's more like I'm helping my mom out, instead of her helping me out. It's her household, so she runs everything.

How old was your mother when you were born?
Twenty-four.

Did she work?
She worked as an administrator, first at the post office, and now for some trade union.

How did she manage to combine working and raising you?
You'd better ask her that! She managed. At that time women could only stay at home for six months after their baby was born. But when I was two, my sister was born, so my mother managed to stay at home until I was four. I didn't even go into day care, as was common then. I went directly to kindergarten. My father also took care of us and my parents lived with my grandparents until I was fifteen. So when I was sick, grandma and grandpa – who were retired – took care of us, and my mother could normally go to work.

If you could have any kind of job or profession, what would it be?
I'd like to be a doctor. I'd enjoy it. But I got married and my husband didn't want me to go to college. But I didn't really have the grades for it. Maybe if I'd really tried I could've passed the entrance exams. But he didn't want me to do it and at that time I was in love with him so I didn't. I started working as a nurse and there was peace between us.

Did you enjoy nursing?
I did enjoy it, and I miss it. I enjoy working with people. And it was interesting – there was always something happening. I know that several girls I used to work with took jobs as waitresses and secretaries, but they have since returned to nursing. They now have less money than before, but they have a job they enjoy. But they are single, without children, so they can afford to work in a field they like.

But I can't afford that, not with a small child. It pays very little and demands a lot of time. As a mother of a three-year-old, I can't work Saturdays or Sundays. Plus I get more money working as a secretary. I work regular hours, from eight to four. I work just across the street from my house. And I get more money than if I worked as a nurse doing shift work.

Do you enjoy your current work?
Not really. It's basically clerical work. Pick up the phone, make the coffee, type something up. Nothing special. And when there's nothing to do – then it's especially boring. I work there so I can have time with my son, so that I don't have to work Saturdays, Sundays, the night shifts. And it's close to where I live.

What was the work like when you were a nurse?
It was very difficult. It demanded a lot, both physically and men-tally. There is a personnel shortage in hospitals, so a lot of the heavy lifting of patients – a job that was supposed to be done by the porters and orderlies – we had to do. The porters and order-lies are men and show me a man who'll work for that kind of pay. Or taking the laundry to the launderers – we also had to do that.

On the psychological side, when you have thirty patients and one nurse – there is always something happening. You're so tired but you can't be rude to the patients. You have to smile at them, chat with them, create a good atmosphere because they're already unhappy because they're in the hospital.

Then there's so much to learn. You come out of school knowing nothing. Eighty per cent of what you know you learn on the job. Every hospital does things a bit differently and practice is very different from theory. I often came home from work so tired that I laid down and went to sleep. In the morning I'd wake up and go to work again. That's not much fun. Now, when I go to sleep, the only thing which can hurt is my back, from sitting all day. Before, when I came back from work, my back hurt because I was pulling old people around the corridors and taking them to the washroom, and turning them over. The work is very poorly rewarded.

Do you have any plans now for your career?
Right now I'm not planning anything. Of course I'd like a better job. At school we studied Russian which is absolutely useless now. So I started taking English. If you want to find a job now, they want you to have at least one language. Other than Russian. First I'll learn English, then maybe I'll learn how to use a computer. Then find a better job. Or if things improved in nursing, I'd return to that.

Improved how?
Financially. And if there were more personnel, so I wouldn't have to wash the floor. If nurses were respected as nurses and not expected to wash the floor and prepare the meals.

Do you think this will happen?
No.

How do you think privatization will change things?
I watch what is going on. But when I see [Health Minister] Rubáš on TV, I turn the TV off. I just can't even look at him.

The whole thing looks to me like they are losing money instead of making it. I think health care should be taken care of by the state. It's not a profit-making venture. It's not right that big hospitals should be put in private hands. Of course, if a doctor wants to open a private practice, that's fine. But big hospitals belong in the hands of the state.

There aren't a lot of rich people among us. And people deserve the best care. Those who take over the hospital are there to make money off it. They're going to offer a lot of expensive services, but only to those who can afford them. And not a lot of people here can afford it. The average person here is looking at whether they can buy an apartment or send their child to a decent school, not worrying over how their heart is working. Their health is the last of their worries. It's bad but that's the way we were raised – to wait until something hurts before we go to the doctor.

What, according to you, are the best and worst things about being a mother?
The best is when the child smiles at you. The worst is that you can't do what you want anymore. You have to take your child into account in everything. You can't just say, 'today I'll go off on my bicycle somewhere'. You have to plan on taking him with you. But I don't see anything terrible in it. I'm glad I have him.

What do you think it means to be a good mother?
I don't know. That's a difficult thing. That's up to the child to judge – when he's eighteen, nineteen, twenty years old, he can say if his mother was good or bad. I try my best to be a good mother. I think about what my mother did, I read about it here and there. But in the end it'll be up to him to say. I try not to neglect him, to introduce him to different things, to spend time with him and take him out into the countryside. But I don't know if I'm doing it right.

What does it mean to be a good father?
I don't know. Probably if he likes the child and the mother. If people are sensible then they can always somehow agree. To like the child and spend at least some time with him is enough.

Who in your opinion should take care of the household?
The husband and wife should agree who should do it, but the primary work is the woman's. She decides what to buy and what's for dinner. Jobs such as figuring out the rent and washing the windows they should divide. All the housework shouldn't fall on one or the other of them – they should divide it. If they are both cleaning up, they will both value that the house is clean. If both of them go shopping, then they won't be swearing at each other for not doing the shopping.

When you were married, did your husband help out with the housework?
Very little. When we first started out we had very little, so there was little to do. Then we got an apartment and I went on maternity leave. I didn't have much money. He made the money. He'd leave at eight in the morning and come home at eight at night, so all the housework was left to me.

Now my mother does the housework. I do about an hour's worth a day – some cooking, ironing, cleaning up. On Saturdays we do a big clean-up that takes longer.

Do you feel any pressure from your parents to stay at home?
I wanted to go to work half a year ago, but my parents wanted me to stay at home with Petr as long as possible. Now that maternity leave has been extended to four years, my parents wanted me to stay that fourth year at home with him. But I couldn't stand it anymore.

Do you want to have more children?
No, I don't want to get married again, and one child is financially difficult enough. I couldn't raise another.

What is your opinion of abortion?
I don't like it but I wouldn't make it illegal. If a woman submits herself to it, then she knows why. I think every normal woman does some hard thinking about whether she wants to keep the child or not. There are a lot of social factors affecting abortion. Young people don't know about contraception, they don't have an apartment, they don't have a good job. So rather than having a sixteen-year-old bring a child into the world into such an uncertain future . . . it's horrible, but I understand it.

Of course, to treat abortion lightly or not use contraception and simply wait for what happens, that's silly. But to make people pay for it is also silly, especially for certain social classes. A Gypsy woman has a lot of kids but can't afford an abortion. She'd rather have the baby and dump it in an orphanage than pay for an abortion. These kinds of people should be provided with free abortions. Otherwise they have twelve children, ten of whom are in orphanages.

Does religion have any influence on your life?
I am not a believer. Of course I believe in some kind of God. But I am afraid of cults. They're expanding here. A number of naive young people are joining the cults and may not end up too good. These cults should be looked into. They should be either banned or there should be fewer of them.

To what extent did you change your ideas and plans after the Velvet Revolution?
I didn't feel much change. Under communism my family did not travel because it wasn't allowed. Now we don't travel because we can't afford it. Under communism my parents supported me. I lived with them and everything seemed normal. Things didn't seem strange or bad. At home my parents said 'don't talk about such-and-such at school', but otherwise when I wanted some candy, I got candy. It's true that when I got older and wanted jeans, we had to go to Tuzex [foreign currency shop]. Now jeans are everywhere and I still can't afford them. Things have changed, but not in a way that really reached me. The revolution occurred when I was still at school. I was on my own only after the revolution.

For me, everything was normal under communism. For me there was no revolution. My life is the same. I can't say it was better before, but it hasn't changed.

Are you content with your life?
Not very much. I imagined it differently. I had ideals before I got married. But it's not as simple as I imagined. But on the other hand I say to myself 'thank God' that I live the way I do. It could've been a lot worse.

If you could change some part of your life, what would you change?
I would live alone. I'd like to have my own apartment and take care of Petr. I'm glad I live with my parents – they help me out a lot – but still, I'm twenty-four years old and for some time I had my own household. I was not used to dealing with my mother's worries, which I have to do now. That's what I'd like – to have my own apartment and be alone with Petr. At this time that's impossible. Even if I had my own apartment, I couldn't manage on my own. But to find some guy just to get an apartment, that's like jumping out of the mud into a puddle. I'd rather stay with my parents.

14 Helena

Helena and I met in her apartment on the outskirts of Prague. The interview took place in her living room which was adorned with paintings, vases, and a large, decorative metal plate on the wall. Helena's toddler-age son was present during the interview and was busily vying for attention. At first, he was crying. Then he was tired and wanted to go to bed. Next he tried to open the box of chocolates I had brought his mother. When she refused to give him all the attention he demanded, he turned to tearing apart the apartment. He attempted to knock the vase of flowers off the table. He tore about a dozen books, including a large collection of loose photographs, off the bookshelf and spilled them out onto the floor. He climbed up onto the couch and tried to pull down the huge metal plate off the wall. Finally, he picked up the tape recorder and tried to bang it against the table.

Helena is a particularly calm and patient mother. She wasn't at all upset by her son's behaviour and did very little to stop him. At one point she very lightly tapped him on the behind and said that he had to stop or she would spank him, but even that was not done in a threatening tone. Unlike many Czech mothers who are generally quick to slap or otherwise physically discipline their children, Helena managed to keep a watchful eye on her son but stayed very calm and relaxed about his behaviour. Perhaps he was more distracting to me than to her, for at times I ended up playing with him through the interview to keep him quiet.

Helena did not say much off tape, except to comment that sometimes she wishes she could have a little girl so she could dress her in frilly dresses and make her look pretty, while her son always looks a bit of a mess. At this point he had a wide, proud grin, complete with mashed cookie crumbs all over his mouth and chin.

Where did your mother work when you were growing up?
With the horses at the race track. She still does it today, but without getting paid. She owns her own horses.

How did she manage to combine her work with raising her children?
We weren't the kind of family that had all our clothes ironed, or a cooked meal three times a day. But it worked.

Was she home a lot?
All three of us rode as a hobby. So after work the whole family was at the tracks and came home only in the evenings. So we did not spend lot of time at home.

Do you think your mother would have preferred to be at home?
Absolutely not. She loves to be outside more than anything else.

Where did your father work?
He also worked at the track. Today he owns a race-horse transportation firm.

Did he help out at home?
I wouldn't say so.

He didn't cook or anything?
Only in emergencies and we had to be in real trouble then.

When did you decide to go to nursing school?
To be honest, only when I found out they took students who had Cs, because I had two of them. Up until then I'd never even been in a hospital. I didn't even know what a nurse's cap looked like. I just wanted to go to a secondary school.

Did you think that one day you'd work as a nurse?
No, not at all. I then had terrible problems. I was once on the children's ward when they removed the child's stitches. It doesn't hurt at all but I still fainted. I felt so sorry for the patients that when they cried out, I fainted onto the floor. It became a problem I couldn't deal with. I could have worked at a clinic, but I don't think I could give someone a shot. I haven't done it in so long . . . and I don't feel drawn to go back to it. I wouldn't want to just be there and do everything the wrong way.

Did you enjoy your education?
It gave me a lot. I gained a completely different outlook on the world. I saw so much pain, so many accidents, that I am now grateful for every day that I spend in comfort. It gave me a lot.

Did you consider any other professions?
At first I wanted to work with horses. But then I decided it was not a job for a girl. It's physically very demanding. And it is to the detriment of her family, and I didn't want that.

Why isn't it good for a girl?
Because I saw that the family isn't the way it should be. And I didn't want that. The nursing school gave me awful lot, I am serious about that. But nursing is not for me. First of all the shifts, then the low pay. I also worked in a kindergarten, but that has nothing to do with health care.

After you finished at nursing school, you went to work in a kindergarten?
No. When I finished school, I was offered, I think it was in 1990, shortly after the revolution, work in Switzerland with horses. So I worked there for almost a year. When I came back, I started to work in a kindergarten. But because I didn't then have a child myself, I couldn't cope very well. I couldn't imagine the responsibility. I had fifteen children four years old, and it was terrible. I couldn't handle it at all. I then took a short accounting course, and looked after my father's books.

Was it interesting work?
I would say so, especially because I was with people I already knew. They were all employees, but I knew them all and we were a good group. It was quite good.

Do you still remember when you were fifteen what you thought you would be doing at twenty-five?
The only thing I knew was that horses would be my destiny till I died. That was the only thing I knew for sure. I have also always wanted to have a child. But otherwise, for example that I will be making my living out of this, that I didn't know. I am at home already a third year, so I want to put my child in day care and go out to work. But I have no idea where and what I will be doing.

But I am going to read advertisements and look for work. I will see what happens.

What would you like to do?
I don't know and I don't really care. I cannot be a nurse because of the shifts. I'm alone now because my husband works abroad. So I can only work in the morning while my son is in day care. I have to pick him up at noon, I cannot leave him at day care from morning till evening. So whatever I can find.

Why do you want to return to work?
Because when I am at home . . . not that I am bored, but. . . . When my son is with other children, he can handle being away from me for three hours. It seems worthless for me to sit idly at home. We have our own horse, so he costs a lot of money. But then my husband's making quite a bit. He's in Berlin now, working with horses. But between me, my son, the apartment, the horse, the dog . . . it isn't easy with money.

When did you get married?
Two years ago.

Can you tell me why you got married?
Because of my mother-in-law and my father-in-law. Our son was already three months old. I didn't want to get married. I was happy just to live together. Because I always said weddings are easier than divorces. That's my opinion. But they kept saying our son would be illegitimate and wouldn't have my husband's name. They kept bothering us, until we finally said yes.

How long has your husband been in Germany?
Three months. He'll be there a long time. He just started his job.

Have you considered joining him there?
I wanted to go. I visit him once a month, for about a week. I leave our son with his grandmother and go. I wanted to get a job there with the horses, but kindergarten there starts only at the age of four, so I wouldn't have anywhere to leave the child. His grandmother offered to take care of him so I could go, but I said it didn't seem very maternal to me to leave without my child.

If you could choose between being at home, working or studying, what would you choose?
I originally wanted to go to college. I borrowed my friend's math textbook to prepare for the exams. I had an A or a B in maths when I left school, so I didn't think I would have any problems with it. But when I opened the book and looked at the first problem, I couldn't even work it half way through. I am so totally out of it, that I gave up. But I'd like to go back to school. It was the nicest time of my life.

What would you like to study?
If I had the brains for it and I could choose, I'd study medicine or veterinary medicine. Or maybe law. But I only said to study, I didn't say to work as a doctor.

When I was at school, I really enjoyed learning about our bodies and everything that goes on. I enjoyed the theory. Even the practice was fine, although I didn't enjoy the hospital. We were always told to imagine what it feels like to be a patient, but I felt it too much. I fainted when we were taking blood. I was always lying on the floor.

What is your opinion of the current changes in the health care system?
I used to argue till very recently that doctors were underrated, and so were nurses. They get very little money yet work all the time. We had arguments about that in my whole family, including my husband, who always claimed that the doctors aren't nearly as good as I say they are. And then just three months ago, my mother got ill. She had a very high fever, and was becoming unconscious. For three days in a row we called the emergency room. They sent someone who gave her Parolen [a Czech equivalent of Tylenol, an analgesic]. Then I came – I was away for part of that time – and found her unconscious. I carried her around the apartment. I called the ambulance who came in forty-five minutes and took her to the hospital. They put her in intensive care and ran some tests. They did a rectal test and then left her with her pants down when she couldn't pull them up. Nobody cared that she was half naked. The only thing they were interested in was her health insurance. Then the next day they called and told me she had meningitis from a tick [a blood-sucking parasite, thought possibly to carry meningitis] and could have easily died. She was half paralysed when I took her there.

They really surprised me. I told the doctor my mother had found a tick on her three weeks earlier. He said that it didn't matter, that it's nothing. But then they found out what it was and they were terrified it might be an infection and spread. Then they were calling every hour. They really made me angry. So I really don't know. They don't make much money . . . but half the people there are so deadened to it all, they don't feel anything.

Why do you think it is so bad?
I don't think it's simply because they make very little money. I think it's the kind of people who are there. I saw that already at school. By the fourth year, a lot of people were quite unfeeling. They were not interested in anything, and did everything mechanically. There was one girl there that the head nurse said could never be a nurse, she was so bad. And today she is one of the five from our class who is still a nurse. She stayed on because she wanted to prove she could do it. I think the attitudes are in the people. They don't value their work. In the health care sector they will take anyone. If I wanted to go back now, they'd take me. But if we had privately owned hospitals and the doctor said that he didn't like how I was behaving, and that I should leave, then I'd rethink how I treat my patients.

How old were you when you got pregnant?
Twenty-one.

How did you feel throughout your pregnancy?
Horribly. For about five months the only thing I could put in my mouth was chicken stock. I was always throwing up. I thought I would die. I didn't show at all. I kept fainting. I walked down Wenceslas Square and vomited on every corner. People stared because they thought I was drunk. It was terrible. I couldn't go through it a second time. The worst part was that I was thin, so you couldn't see anything.

And then it got better?
Yes, after the fifth month, I felt perfect. And I was hungry! Eleven dumplings were not a problem for me.

What do you remember from the birth?
I wouldn't say it made me want to go through it again. But I had a great doctor and great nurses. I was lucky in that the ward had

been closed the week before to be repainted. I was the first mother when it reopened and I was there alone. The nurses had had a week off, and so had the doctor. They were still so radiant they sat with me the whole time. They didn't leave me alone.

Do you want to have more children?
Yes. I'd like to have a girl when my son gets older. I admire mothers who have twins or triplets. I don't know what I'd do.

What do you think is a good age for a woman to have her first child?
I think before she's twenty-seven or twenty-eight. Then it's very late. Everywhere abroad they say to start at thirty. But then when the child is ten, the mother is forty. I can't imagine her going ice skating with the child or going swimming or skiing or playing with him. She'd be the kind of mother who would say, 'go play with your friends'. I try to have a more comradely relationship with my son. To be friends rather than to have authority and put my child down.

Do you think it is different to raise a son than a daughter?
I don't think so. I always thought it was but now I see that my son is very sensitive, like girls usually are. So I don't think there are so many differences until they get older but I'll find out if I have a girl.

For you what is the best part and the worst part of being a mother?
The best part is that, at least now when he is young, I am the greatest in his eyes. He loves me unconditionally. He doesn't hold anything against me. He loves me just the way I am.

And the worst? I don't know – I don't think there is anything at all bad about it. Women are born in order to have children. Not to have careers. I think you can manage both. But I don't understand women who never have children, who don't want children.

What is bad about that?
I don't know. I just believe that women are born to have children and families. Not to build things. That's my personal opinion.

And what about men who don't have children?
You can always find another man to have children with. But I don't even know any persons who don't want children. I don't mean in

their twenties but at some point in their lives. My aunt had her first child at forty. I don't think that's an ideal age, but at least she has him.

I always thought about horses, horses. I thought about my career . . . and then when my son was born, I realized that I hadn't even lived before I had him. I look at life completely differently now.

Is motherhood what you expected it to be?
It's better than I thought. But not always. Of course there are moments when I think, 'Dear God, can't he just disappear somewhere?' But otherwise, it's good.

Who in your opinion should take care of the housework?
It depends on the situation. If we have two weeks holiday and we are both being couch potatoes in front of the TV, then we should divide the work. But if the husband leaves home at 6 a.m. and returns at 6 p.m., his wife can't expect him to help out when she is home all day. But if she works from six to six, they should split it.

What would you think if a man stayed home with the kids and his wife worked?
I would like that. However, my husband would never do it! He spends five minutes with his son and he gets nervous because our son is very wild. But otherwise, I have nothing against such a setup, because a father is a father. But I wouldn't leave him with a stranger.

When he is around, does your husband help out with the housework?
He tries to.

What does he do?
He would do just about anything. But he washes the dishes in such a way that there are bits of egg stuck on them. I'd rather do it myself. He makes an effort but he wasn't born to do it, so I usually strategically kick him out – otherwise I have to do it all over again.

How much of your time does housework take up?
The whole day. Since I'm here all day, I'm always doing something so I don't get lazy. Before, when there were just the two of us, it was different. We didn't need much. We'd go out to a restaurant for dinner.

But with my son . . . at first I didn't cope at all. I didn't expect it to be so much work. I didn't have any experience with diapers and so on. Now it's better. In two years I've learned how to get it all done. I have a system off pat, but my husband does everything backwards as it suits him, so it takes him twice as long. But we'll see how it goes when I go back to work, if I can handle it all.

Who do you think is better off in life, men or women?
I think girls are better off. Guys go to school, do their military service, and then have to work the rest of their lives. But a girl has a much more varied life. She has a child, then goes back to work. Then maybe has another child. And they experience maternal love. A father can really love his child but he can never know what it's like to give birth.

Does religion have any influence in your life?
I am a believer, but in my own way. I believe that something exists. . . . I believe in life after death. But I don't belong to a particular religion. I have my own principles that I try to uphold.

Do you think it is important for your son to learn about religion?
I would not mind if they had religion at school. He should know something about it. In my view, this belongs to the classical education everybody should have. But if he believes in it or not is his own decision. Yet he should know about it, its history, and so on. That always comes handy.

To what extent did you change your plans or ideas following the Velvet Revolutoin?
I was never interested in politics. When the other girls came and told me they were at a strike rally on Wenceslas Square that day, I thought 'What were they doing there? They would only get beaten up.' I am very conservative in these things. I didn't really experience the revolution. I accepted that things changed, but I didn't really care. The only difference, I guess, is that people can now start their own businesses.

I was a Sparklett, a pioneer and a member of the youth union.[1] I have never wanted to have a career in politics. I felt the same way after the revolution. I don't care.

Did your life change at all?
Only in so far as it is now possible to become an entrepreneur. My whole life I've known that I'll have to have some kind of a job, and that horses will be my hobby. After the revolution, I realized that I could have the horses as my employment. I mean my own horses.

Is that an important change for you?
Financially speaking – yes. The way our family used to live before and how we live now is extremely different. We could've only dreamed about this.

NOTE

1. Based on the Soviet model, these were communist children's and youth organizations. Although membership was not compulsory, practically everybody belonged, especially the younger age groups. Sparkletts catered to children aged 6–9, pioneers to 10–15 years old, and the youth organization covered anybody over the age of 15 and under the age of 35.

15 Renata

When Renata and I met, she wanted to get down to the questions right away. Once the interview was over, she was friendly but didn't seem very interested in continuing the conversation beyond the 'official' questions. Off tape, she discussed her current job a little more, speaking generally about problems with discipline, mood changes, and violence among mentally disturbed children. She was dressed in a knee-length skirt and hose, and repeatedly laughed and pointed out the runs where they had been tugged on by the children. While she enjoys her work, she acknowledged that it might be very difficult to stay in this position for more than a short time.

I grew up until the age of six with both my parents. Then my father died in a car accident, so it was just me, my younger brother, and our mom.

My mom has worked for the last twenty years at a water treatment facility. She's an engineer, a project manager and a head of a department there. She is quite happy at her workplace. She always thought that she would leave, but after the revolution, water treatment has become cost-effective. There is lot of talk about the need for clean air and water, so from an ecological perspective, being in water treatment is quite good. They have just approved a project to build the largest water treatment facility in Prague, so that there is enough clean water for all of Prague.

How do you think she managed to combine raising her family with having a job?
She managed it very well, despite the fact she was alone. Her work is very demanding. She has a lot of responsibility. But me and my brother never felt she was just taking care of us financially. She made our childhoods wonderful. I can only hope to be just as good.

When did you decide to go to nursing school?
When we had to fill out our high school applications, I couldn't think of anything else. I thought it would be nice. I liked the idea

of a uniform. I was so young! I thought it would be nice to wear a cap. But it was more by accident. Nothing else came to mind. I wasn't a good enough student to go to a regular academic high school.

When I was in 8th grade I told myself it would be good if I got married soon and had a lot of kids. I played with infants, changed their diapers. So maybe I wanted to go to nursing school to be near children. I don't remember having any dreams of who I could be. I just accepted what came. I accepted that I was in nursing school and would be a nurse.

What kind of work do you do now?
I spent five years working in a hospital but now I work at the Centre for Children and Families. As a facility for child psychiatry, it caters to children from socially disadvantaged families or from families where their parents didn't take care of them, because they are even more stupid than their kids. Or it caters to kids who misbehave so badly that they couldn't be in a regular class-room with thirty children. There is a psychologist, a psychiatrist, and various other care-givers at the Centre. I started off as a care-giver but now I'm a teacher. There are five teachers there. I do not have the required qualifications but I have applied to the education faculty. I was short five points. I was not accepted. I'll apply again next year because I can only work there for two years without the teaching qualification. Now I'm taking introductory courses in education to prepare me for the university level courses once I actually get accepted into the programme.

I'd like to get the training and stay at this job. At times it is very hard. Even though I teach only eight kids, they really misbehave. They don't listen. They jump out of the windows. They fight, beat each other up. But then again I only teach from eight in the morning to noon, so four hours is bearable. It's also very flexible. We can take breaks whenever we decide the kids are tired. Or we can take them outside or give them a snack or sing a song together. Or just relax with them to some music.

The children need us. They need to know somebody likes them. That somebody is willing to listen to them when they have a problem. These are kids whose parents beat them and abuse them. They might, for example, lock them in a room and leave them there all day. So the children are anxious and frightened. They express it by misbehaving, by venting their anger on others.

I'm there to teach them, but we spend only about fifteen minutes on lessons. Otherwise we tell stories. I tell them basic things about how to act and how a normal family should look. How they should wash their hands and eat with a fork. Sometimes I feel very sorry for them. They can misbehave terribly, but still, their souls are sensitive. Nobody ever loved them.

These kids no longer live with their families?
Some are in the Centre for about three months for treatment. Over the week they are with us, but on the weekends they go back to their parents. You can easily tell after they've been with us for three months. We can't reform them completely but we have shown them the way. They then return to their families and things go back to the way they were. At times I wonder if there is a point to it all. But I think there is. I hope so.

Do you live with your family?
No. I rented a sub-let flat for a while. Then I got kicked out because the owner found out. So I moved back home for two months. Then I got another sublet from a friend who went to America for a year and half, but I just found out that she is coming back and I have to move again. It is such an awful problem finding a place to live. Sometimes I think I'll be wandering the streets with my backpack until I'm eighty, looking for a place to rest my head. I'd say this is my biggest problem – that I have three months to find a place to live.

Who do you think is better off in life, men or women?
I don't know. I'm glad I'm a woman. I wouldn't want to be a guy, but then again I'm sure a guy is glad to be a guy.

Why wouldn't you want to be one?
It just seems clear to me that I'm a girl. I never thought about what it would be like to be a boy. I'm glad I'm a woman. I like it. A guy has to be decisive and self-aware and know what he's doing. But a woman – she can let guys advise her. She doesn't need to be totally independent. She knows she has someone to lean on.

Do you want to have children?
Yes.

When?
I'm at the point that if I met the right guy, I could start a family right away. Maybe I'm already thinking when I meet someone if he would be the right person to have a family with. It depends on when I meet him. It could be now or in five years.

When you have children, would you like to stay at home with them?
Of course. For a long time. I couldn't face putting them in day care and kindergarten. I'd like to stay at home until they are at least five years old.

How many kids do you want to have?
I'd like to have a lot, have a big family, so that we'll have a big kitchen table and lots of people around it. Definitely more than two kids. I still have my fantasy of having eight, I'd like that.

What do you think it means to be a good mother?
It's very demanding to be a good mother. I'd like to be able to handle it. It should be possible. If a person wants to have a family, she should be a good mother. A mother and her child should have the kind of relationship where they can tell each other anything. Where they can be open and upfront. Where the child knows she can come to her mother and tell her anything. Her mother should always have time to be with her, to caress her and be kind to her. She should explain everything to her and treat her with a lot of care. This relationship should last all the way until the mother is eighty years old. I think it's difficult to have such a relationship but I hope that I'll be able to handle it. I'd very much like to be able to handle it.

And to be a good father?
That's hard for me to imagine because I grew up just with my mom. I had a period when I thought I'd be a single mother. I thought it would be very nice to be alone with two kids who would love me, and that I'd be able to handle it. I knew that a family could function with just a mother. But now I think I wouldn't want it that way. A complete family must be good. I just can't imagine it.
When you look at many families, you see that in lot of marriages the people are married, but they aren't faithful to each other. At times I really don't know what's better – a mother alone with

her kids or a family where there's a father on paper but he's never there. But I think a father should be the kind of person you can rely on and who will take care of his family, love them all, and whom they all love in return.

Do you think it's different to raise a daughter than a son?
Absolutely. There's a different relationship between fathers and their daughters and fathers and their sons. I was always envious of girls who have a father. I think the relationship between a mother and a son or a father and a son is very nice. It's different from raising a daughter. But I'm not sure I can say how.

What in your opinion are the advantages and disadvantages of not having children?
There are no advantages. I can't see a single one. I think it's very sad not to have children. Within all women there is something maternal that makes it so that she must have children. If it doesn't work out and for some reason she doesn't have them, she can act like she is fine, but I think it's very sad. I know I would be very unhappy and I feel sorry for such people. So I don't see any advantages. I think it's great when one has a family where everything is functioning well.

Does religion have any influence on your life?
I don't go to church regularly and I'm not an orthodox believer. But I do think that there exists somewhere another power and that there are definitely more lives than this one. I don't know if that's 'religion' in the proper sense, but more a question of belief. But I wouldn't say it has a major impact on my life.

When you have children, do you want to raise them within a religion?
Definitely. I want to take them to church and show them what it is about. It's up to them what they decide to do with that knowledge. When we were small, I loved to go to church with my grandmother. I loved the singing and I loved being there. It's nice when a person explains religion to a child and then when the child is older, it's up to them if they want to believe or just think about such things. But I wouldn't compel my children to accept a certain faith because I am not clear about it myself.

Are you interested in politics?
Very generally. I know who is the president and who is who in politics. I was very interested in politics during the revolution. I read all the papers and knew everything that was going on. Since then I've kept up with the basic issues, but I cannot say that I explore them too deeply or argue over them. That seems like a waste of time.

To what extent has your life changed since the Velvet Revolution?
I was just about to graduate when it happened. I was just entering into the world as things changed, so to me it seems completely normal that things are the way they are now. Before the revolution I wasn't interested in politics. But when there was the revolution I realized how it was before, and what a lot of new opportunities there are now.

Before the revolution, politics was irrelevant to me. I knew what things were like and that I couldn't change them. I had to live with them, so I thought I would. So before I entered the workforce, everything changed. Now it seems to me that it was always like that.

Do you have more opportunities now?
Definitely. I have more opportunities to realize my potential. Before, you could have potential but you had to hide it in a drawer. Now, whatever you resolve to do – if you want it and have the power to go for it – you can do it.

What do you hope for in the future?
I hope to meet a person with whom I can start a family. I hope to keep the friends I have, not to lose any. I hope that everything goes well at the Centre and that we have enough money for the school to run well. And I hope I find a place to live!

16 Zdena

Zdena arranged for us to meet at her favourite restaurant in the centre of town. She had already cancelled one interview, and when she didn't show up in the first half hour, I gave up on her. I ordered some lunch and sat back with my newspaper. But she came running in forty minutes late, apologizing that she'd been kept late at work at the hospital.

Immediately she began to talk about her thoughts on health care, her work, and what she expected from the interview. Then she suddenly stopped and asked me if she was speaking too much and would I rather wait for her to answer my specific questions. When I shook my head, she took off again. Out of all the interviewees, she was the one who most clearly knew what she wanted to say and steered the interview in her own direction. She is also the only one who responded affirmatively to the closing question of 'is there anything else you would like to add?'

Zdena's appearance was also strikingly different from most of the other interviewees. She has a large, broad face, and short-cropped hair. She was dressed very casually and did none of the general things that most of the interviewees do to look more traditionally 'feminine' – no makeup, no smart clothes, no long, dyed hair. She smiled a lot, and was extremely friendly. She also stood out for making eye contact for a long time. She struck me as a very direct and honest person, who had no interest in pretending to be someone she is not.

After the tape recorder was turned off, Zdena chatted some more about her boyfriend. She described him as very athletic and encouraging of her to get more involved in sports. She had started cycling with him and his male friends and remarked that sometimes she finds herself sitting with them in a pub, and realizes how strange it is that she is the only woman there. She gave the impression of often being in the company of men.

She was not very curious about her classmates whom I had interviewed, which also sets her apart from the majority of interviewees. (She did say that she is not surprised that so many of the women in her class are no longer nurses and that she cannot explain why she's stayed in nursing except that it somehow 'suits her'.) She also did not ask me much about myself and had none of the usual 'what is life

like in America' questions. Unlike most of the other women, she seemed
quite comfortable talking about herself without opening up other avenues
of discussion.

I was born in Moravia. I was about three years old when we moved
to Prague and I've lived here ever since. I have one sister who is
now eighteen. She's already married and is expecting a baby in
about a month.

When we lived in Moravia my mother worked at a shoe factory.
I was born when she was twenty-two. She spent two years at home
with me. My dad, I cannot remember what he did. Now he works
for the Prague construction company. He blasts tunnels needed to
build the subways.

My parents got divorced when I was nine years old. I lived with
my mother after that.

Was she happy with her work when you were a child?
In those days there was almost nothing else. She could've been a
shop assistant. Her family had no money for studying. My grandmother got widowed quite early. My mother's father died when
she was fifteen. After that, she had to go straight to work to support her family because there were also two sisters. She could've
worked in a store, or in some small firm or in that factory. There
were not a lot of choices.

Do you think she ever wished to stay at home as a housewife?
I don't think so. It wouldn't have interested her. After my sister
was born, she soon returned to work. She didn't want to be at
home. In any case, it wasn't possible for her to stay at home even
when she still lived with my father. She never said that she wished
to be a housewife, we never talked about that.

How did she manage to combine her job with raising you?
I think she handled it well. She often said that she was tired, but it
didn't affect us. We didn't lose out on anything. Even when she
got divorced, she still managed everything. We never felt like we
didn't have enough money or something like that.

Did she have enough time for you?
She did. She never told us she didn't have time for us. She went on walks with us to the park or to the zoo. I am not aware that she was suffering in any way.

And did your father spend time with you?
Not really. At first when I was very young I didn't really notice it that much. They got divorced when I was nine, so I didn't really remember him that much. I remember one thing. When I started school, he bought me my first school bag. That's the only thing I remember about him from when I was a kid.

When did you decide to become a nurse?
In 8th grade when we were choosing secondary schools. I didn't have the grades for a secretarial school, and in any case, I didn't think I'd like to sit in an office all day. When I looked through the list of schools, nothing struck me. So I went to nursing school. If I could choose again, I'd study something that would benefit me, that would give me something. I'd like to learn how to sew so maybe I'd study to be a seamstress. Something like that.

I don't get much out of nursing. I'd like to be able to do something for myself. I enjoy nursing and can't imagine that I would do something else. But it exhausts me too much, both physically and mentally. It's terribly demanding and I would like to have something simpler. I am looking wherever I can. I would like to study but I don't know if it is possible. I'd like to get a baccalaureate. Or a nursing speciality. Or study to be a midwife. Usually it takes two years to get a baccalaureate, oh but the entrance exams! I'm afraid of them. Just to get through biology . . .!

Can you say why you picked nursing in the first place?
I don't know why. I guess I didn't really know what I was getting into. I just chose what sounded interesting – to learn about the body. I am collecting books, and I have at home several about the human body, and I'm interested in how it all works. I've always been interested in studying that. But I only found out what nursing is about when I started working. And I do enjoy it.

What are the best and worst parts of your job?
The best is when I go home! I work a lot with cancer patients. Young people who are very ill. Most of them are dying. It's really

awful and it takes a lot out of me to watch a young person die. That's the bad side of the job. But sometimes we manage to have fun, especially with the elderly women patients. I prefer older people as patients than the younger ones. When I know they are ill at twenty . . . that's bad.

If you could have any kind of profession, or stay at home, what would you choose?
I'd go to school. I'd like to have an education, go to work and be independent. I wouldn't want to be at home with children and a husband. I plan to have a family, but not right now. More likely when I'm thirty.

Why thirty?
That's the age when I might want to have children. Right now I don't want them. I don't have enough money. But I'm only twenty-three and I don't think I need to have them so soon. I'd like to be free and independent. I'd like to travel somewhere.

Are you married?
No.

Are you in a serious relationship with anybody?
Oh yes. We've been going out for three years. Occasionally somebody tells me that when you're together three years you should either marry each other or split up. But we talked about it and decided we don't want to get married yet.

Do you feel any pressure from your family?
No. My sister just got married so my mother is busy with her. She doesn't care about it at all. She looks after the dog. She has a house outside of Prague. She takes care of the garden. She is quite indifferent to what I do here. We call each other, but we don't see each other much. She does what she does and I do what I do.

What do you think it means to be a good mother?
To devote yourself to the child and raise her well. To encourage the good in her. To teach her about nature, not to sit at home in front of a video or computer. I wouldn't allow them to do that. To show them how to have good relationships with people. But I wouldn't shower them with unquestioning love, like some monkey. I'd want

to be the way our mom was with us. She didn't have a lot of money to shower us with presents. But we had a nice environment. We went on trips. I'd try to do it the same way.

And a good father?
He is behind the family, interested in his kids, not sitting in a bar all evening. My boyfriend does a lot of sports, especially bike racing, so it'd be nice if he taught the kids that, so they aren't loafing about all the time. He should spend time with them.

Do you remember back when you were fifteen, what you thought you would be doing at twenty-three?
I never really thought then about what I'd be doing when I got older. I thought about where I was going to go to school, things like that. The future didn't interest me.

I didn't even plan to date anyone. I thought that I'd be single, not that I'd be in a serious relationship. I thought I'd be going out to the disco and doing things like that.

Most of the people at work are young. For the most part the girls don't have boyfriends. They go out, buy what they want, enjoy their freedom. I'm already a little bit out of it, because I have a boyfriend. I can't go wherever I want, I need to work things out with him. For them it's different and sometimes I envy that. But then again, they're telling me that they are envious of me since I have such a nice boyfriend.

How many jobs have you had since you finished school?
I'm still at the same job I had after graduation. I haven't changed jobs, but I do think about it now that it's been five years.

Why do you want a different job?
Mainly because I am emotionally tired from it. I'd like a calmer job, a different group of people. I'm fine with the other nurses, but some of the doctors.... They behave dreadfully towards us. I'd like a place where I would feel differently.

Did your education prepare you for your job?
No. It was absolutely inadequate. The education was quite superficial, I didn't learn what I really needed to know for the job. I didn't learn the practical clinical side at all! Going once a week to the hospital did not teach me what I know now. At school we covered

a little bit of everything so we ended up knowing nothing. So you had to relearn it all when you started working. Even basic skills. I did not learn those from the school clinical practice. I learned them only subsequently, after I came to work at the hospital.

I would change a lot in the curriculum. Within six months of enrolling, I'd take the students to the hospital and show them how it really is there. I know that the cost would be that a lot of them would quit. They'd see how we are run off our feet, and how little money we get. I'd also show them right from the beginning how to deal with patients. I wouldn't leave it until the third year! In the third year many girls step into the hospital and realize they don't like it, it's nothing like the classroom. So I'd introduce them to the patients straight away. I'd eliminate some of the theoretical lectures. There is too much theory. Better they get hands-on experience with the patients. They are going to spend the rest of their lives with them.

What is your opinion of the current transformation of the health care system?
It's very bad. It would appear that I'm a pessimist. It's a very bad system. The insurance companies pay too late. If you order something in the hospital, it takes a long time to arrive, people lie in bed a whole day waiting for their medicines. If we had computers in the wards and we could order medication through them, it would lighten our load considerably. Things would certainly speed up. Now you have to make a mark on a patient's chart for every shot you give them. Then you add up the marks and work out the sum that the insurance company owes you. Somebody has to sit there adding up marks instead of improving the whole system.

Today's doctors care only about money and about getting bigger salaries. I don't think that they care about the patients at all. I don't trust them and I wouldn't strike for them.

The cost of medication is very high. Doctors are prescribing medications that are too expensive. Hospitals can't make any money when people don't co-pay. An old man lies in the hospital for nearly a month. At home he's getting his pension; it is nicely being put in the bank while the hospital is shelling out money on him. When you're at home you have to pay for your electricity, heat and food. In the hospital, patients don't have to pay for anything. And the insurance companies don't give us enough either.

What kind of voice should nurses have in the changes that are occurring?

Nurses' role should be made more visible because the doctors treat us like a piece of dirt. They don't treat us like nurses, but like some janitors. We get no status, no prestige. Nobody respects that I'm a nurse.

About the economics of running a hospital, I don't know much. I can't worry about it when I'm responsible for caring for the patients. But I know that sometimes we are caring for people who don't even want to be there. You take care of an alcoholic who walks out and has another drink, and it becomes a vicious circle and we are paying for his care. It's money out of our pockets, and it really angers me. These people shouldn't be there, or else should be paying for their care. Or their health insurance should be more expensive than for me, who neither smokes nor drinks. There should be some sanction for self-induced illness, caused by, say, drugs, etc. Instead a doctor orders them to go for treatment. Sometimes they welcome the opportunity to be somewhere where it's warm, they get three meals a day, and someone makes their bed for them. What else do they need? They are happy to be there and they don't even pay a crown a day. A person like that never wants to leave.

Do you think that nursing should become more open to male nurses?

No, I don't think men should be nurses. They should be ambulance drivers who help out the nurses with lifting patients or moving heavy people. We have people like that, but not enough of them. But then it's natural for nobody to want to do that kind of job. But when it comes to taking care of patients, I don't think men should do that. It's women's work. Men are good for heavy work but not if you have to take care of women patients, especially when you have to take care of their bodily needs. The women patients wouldn't let a man do that.

Do you mean things such as bathing them?

Yes, things like that. And I can understand it. Someone might say they wouldn't mind a man. After all he sees women every day on a pinup or at home naked. But in a hospital? I personally wouldn't like it if some young boy came to nurse me.

Do you belong to any professional nursing associations?
No. No associations. I think they are worthless. I'm sick of how we always had to be members of some kind of organization. Take the Red Cross. I joined it the minute I started nursing school. They never sent me to any meetings. Nothing ever came out of it. So I'm not interested. I don't want to be in any groups, any associations, anything like that.

Where do you live?
I live with my boyfriend in my parents' apartment. My parents don't live there, but it's still their apartment, it's got all their furniture. So I can't change the apartment around much unless I first get my mother's approval, which isn't hard. If I say to her that I want this to be purple, she'll nod her head and it's going to be purple. But it is still very much their apartment. It would be great if we could buy it from them and it would then be ours.

What is your boyfriend's occupation?
Karel drives a bus, a normal public bus in Prague. He sometimes works the night shift or weekends, so sometimes I don't get to see him much. He comes back from work just as I'm leaving. And when he's off, he has to train for his bicycle races, so it is difficult.

When you have children, do you plan on staying at home with them?
As long as possible. Yes. As long as I can afford to. But at least until they are going to school. At least until they are about six. Maternity benefits last four years, but I'd like to stay those extra two. It depends on the financial situation. If it's not possible, I'd go back to work.

What is your opinion of day care?
Day care? I used to visit day-care facilities when I was at nursing school. I think they take good care of children there. They play with them. Even if the child plays by itself, it can learn self-reliance, it can learn how to eat by itself. At home if the child doesn't want to eat, its mother doesn't know what to do. But in day care, it sees the five kids next to it eating and it learns. Definitely day care is good for people who don't know what to do with their kids when they have to go to work. If I had to, I'd definitely put my child there.

Do you think a father can take as good care of a child as a mother?
Absolutely.

If you were married and were working, and your husband offered to stay at home with the kids, what would you say?
If the child was just a baby, then no. But maybe after a year it would be OK. If my husband wanted it, then I'd happily change places with him. The child would develop a relationship to his father. He wouldn't just see him in the evenings when he comes home from work. My cousins had it like that. They hardly ever saw their father because by the time he came home from work, they were asleep.

I think a man could stay at home with the kids. Some men could take better care of them than some women. They can cook and clean. I think they should trade off.

Does your boyfriend help you with the housework?
He helps a lot. When he feels like it, he does a lot. He irons, vacuums, washes the windows. But he can't cook. We've been together for three years and only once have I gotten breakfast in bed. He won't even butter a slice of bread for me. If he's hungry, he just buys a roll. He wouldn't even heat up a sauce or anything. But otherwise he'll help out with any kind of men's work in the house, even vacuuming.

Who in your opinion should take care of the housework?
It depends on the situation. It's more in the woman's domain, but if for some reason she can't do it, it's not stated anywhere that the man has to earn the money and the woman has to be at home with the kids. If a woman earns more than a man, then she should go to work and he can take care of the children. I think they should share the work. Some older people are rooted in the idea that this is men's work and this is women's work and they won't touch the other person's jobs. I think that's stupid. They should do the work together.

Who do you think is better off in life, men or women?
Definitely men. They can spend all day reading the newspaper if they want. But a woman – she has responsibilities. She has to take care of the children and cook for them. If the man doesn't want to do it, then it's left up to her.

In many couples I know, mainly older couples, the man does men's work and the woman women's work. They don't split it. And the man ends up with fewer responsibilities. But I think they should decide who does what. But definitely men have it better.

What is classical men's work?
Chopping wood. Well, no . . . going to work. It depends on where you live. If you live in a house he has to take care of it, make sure the roof isn't leaking and there is something to heat it with. A woman, on the other hand, washes the windows and cooks. If they live in an apartment, they have less work to do.

Does religion have any influence on your life?
No. I'm an atheist, an active atheist, I don't go to church. I might say, 'Dear God, what are you punishing me for?' That's just a saying to make a person feel better. But I'm not interested in God.

I felt very uncomfortable when my cousin had a wedding in a church. I had no idea how to act. I'd never been in a church before. I didn't know if I was supposed to stand or sit or if I was supposed to sing. It was very uncomfortable.

What is your opinion on abortion?
Abortion is a terrible thing, but a woman should always be able to count on it as a last resort. If she doesn't want to have a child, she shouldn't have one.

Abortions shouldn't happen. Definitely not in the conveyor-belt fashion they happen now. But it should always be an option. It's democratic right for her to have such an option. Otherwise, she should use contraception. Abortion should be the last resort.

Would you ever work in a ward that did abortions?
Yes, a person is a person whatever they come in for. But I think it's difficult for a woman to have an abortion. At the time she might not be aware of it, but then a month later she realizes what she's done. But then she is no longer at the hospital . . .

Do you think there should be any laws governing abortion?
It definitely should not be made illegal. Definitely not. But it should be fixed so that not every woman who thinks of it can just get one right away. She should have to discuss it with a psychologist, have some chance to think it over. But to make abortion illegal is ridiculous

because it will just be done illegally. There have always been abortions, and there always will be.

Are you interested in politics?
Not much. There are some things that irritate me. For example, that they are going to start a senate, which is completely worthless since we already have a parliament. On numerous occasions I'd like to throw a bomb into the parliament. They really irritate me, the things they do, like voting themselves a salary increase while I work here for 5000 crowns [monthly salary US $192]. They even get to ride public transit for free. But I wouldn't say I'm interested in politics. I can't change anything anyway. I didn't even vote. Maybe when I'm older, I'll care enough to. But now . . . how many young people vote?

Why would it be different when you're older?
I'll be more responsible for what is happening here, and I'll vote in the 'better' candidates. I'll be more responsible for how things will be for my kids. But now, I'm not interested.

What about improving things for yourself?
I don't think things will change. My voice is not important in an election. A single individual can't change things. In some ways, the majority of things are still the same as they were under the communists. I still don't get asked if they're going to build a petrol station on the corner. Nobody cares if I want it there or not. The communists never asked. They did what they wanted. Now we are ruled by money. Those who have money have it all. In some ways, it's very cruel. If you have money, you can build a house. Other people couldn't care less that you're living in some horrible apartment with a leaking roof. We are ruled by money and I don't like it. There are things I'd change. But of course, I don't want the communists back.

To what extent did your life change following the Velvet Revolution?
The thing I like the most is that now the shops are full of goods. I can window-shop from morning till evening and look at beautiful things. That's what struck me the most about the revolution because I was only seventeen. That there was a fight over power and control – I didn't get that part. I liked seeing the things in the

shops and being able to go to Germany and generally travel. But I don't have enough money to travel, even though I'd really like to.

I know that now we can say whatever we want to. But it's democracy all over the place. So now we have on every street corner a prostitute, an illegal money-changer, and a taxi driver who never pays his taxes. And I have to support this. I don't like it, but it's democracy.

Do you have more prospects now?
No, I can't say that. But I'm glad it happened. I'm glad I can go and buy whatever I want, travel, or study. Before, if the authorities decided that I could not go to that school, they didn't give me permission and I couldn't go. Now, when I take the entrance exams, I have a chance of being accepted. In everyday life, the prospects are better in some ways and worse in others. I definitely don't like the rise in brutality. On TV you have shooting and killing in every film. But you can't change that, not even by voting. I cannot do anything about that by myself.

Would you say you are content with your life?
Oh yes. I'm healthy and that's for me by far the most important thing. When I see those young people dying at work.... For me there is nothing more important than to be healthy. And for my parents too.

I have some money and I can support myself. It's quite simple.... I mean on the level that's available to me. I don't have millions, so I can't say I have it made. But within limitations, I am completely happy. I have a kind boyfriend, a place to live, a bit of money, friends, and my health. I don't need anything else. I don't need millions.

What do you wish for from the future?
That things will get better. But I think it's empty words to think that way! I'd like there to be justice for everyone – but those are silly things to talk about. I guess I want to be healthy, to have healthy children, and for my parents to be healthy. I want things to be the way they are, and not to get worse. Every once in a while I hear something about Russia and I fear that the Russians will tear in here and start World War III. I imagine I'll have kids, they'll grow up and I'll lose them to drugs. So why have them? But there's no way to influence such things.

I just sometimes wonder what it is all for. Now I enjoy myself and spend my money but where will it take me in the future? What will things be like here? At night I watch the TV news and it's full of murders, accidents, wars in the Third World, natural catastrophes, and earthquakes. I get very pessimistic and think, 'what is all this for?' A factory could explode. There could be a fire or a chemical leak. We live only as long as we live. And the future . . .?

Those are all the questions I wanted to ask you. Do you have anything you'd like to add?
Back to the government. There are a lot of things that could be changed.

Politically?
Perhaps I get irritated that I live in Prague but I can't affect what goes on here. I get really irritated that there's a petrol station on every street corner. I'd like to have a voice in deciding these things. In what gets built. In various laws. Like the restitution laws. People ask for their land back and get it.[1] But what about the people who lived there the last forty years. What happens to them? And what if it's a young family? I don't like it.

I'd like to be able to influence these decisions. Maybe through a referendum, or in some other way. But these are such Bohemian aspirations that they are almost unreachable.

When you vote for the government, that doesn't influence things?
No. Even if you elected a different party, they'd still do things you wouldn't like. They'll always do things you don't like.

But perhaps some are better than others?
No. I think they are all the same, better in some things, worse in others. I also think that if this party is already in power, it should stay in power. If we are rushing forward in one direction, it doesn't make sense to change parties and speed ahead in a different direction. Then we'll always be in the same place. We should go in one direction until we get somewhere. Replacing cabinet ministers or changing parties doesn't lead you anywhere. It's not like I think the communists should've stayed. I don't mean that at all. But now that elections are coming up [on 1 June 1996] if they vote in someone else, God knows where they will lead us.

What do you think would be the best solution?
When you vote somebody in, leave them in. After that you should have referendums so you can influence the people in parliament. I don't agree that Parliament should be full of old men who are half asleep and hardly ever go there, but get paid for it. I don't want them representing me. If there is, for example, a proposed law to make smoking in public illegal, I want them to approve it. I don't want them to brush it off the table and disagree with it.

Or to sit in the apartment smoking?
Yes! You said it. And I don't agree with them sitting there doing nothing. I want a system where every person can make up their mind and have it actually count.

NOTE

1. Zdena is referring to the restitution law passed in the aftermath of the Velvet Revolution. This law made it possible for residents whose property was confiscated after 1948 by the communist authorities to get it back.

17 Implications and Analysis: A New Generation in the Making?

Having read the fourteen interviews, the reader is invited to draw his or her own conclusions. In this final chapter, our aim is to outline our own perspective on the data. Our analysis is based not only on the interviews presented in this book, but also on the nine interviews not included in the book.

We would like to argue that the relationship of Czech women to work both inside and outside of the home is more complex than has often been asserted; that the rhetoric of individualism is crucial to understanding the world-views of young Czech women, and that the 1989 revolution had profound consequences not only on the ways in which they live their lives, but also on the ways in which they see themselves.

GENDER AND MOTHERHOOD

Numerous researchers, both Western and Czech, have argued that since the 1989 revolution there has been a return to traditional gender roles in the Czech Republic. Czech women are retreating into the home, the argument goes, valuing the role of housewife over that of worker, and ignoring careers for the privacy of the domestic sphere. A recent example of this line of thinking can be found in Matynia (1995, p. 386), who argues that 'one of the most puzzling trends in post-1989 Czechoslovakia has been the expressed desire of women to withdraw from the world of work into the world of the household, domesticity and the family'. In a similar vein, Wolchik (1992) notes that during the 1990 electoral campaign, representatives from all the political parties agreed that mothers with small children should remain at home to care for them. The emphasis on a woman's need to realize her 'feminine nature' through domesticity is similar to the argument put forward by reformers during the 1968 'Prague Spring', when sending women home and saving on day care was considered a progressive demand (Heitlinger, 1995).

As we hope to show in this final chapter, the interviews in this book point to a more complex relationship between the domestic and the public spheres. While the domestic sphere is valued as a space of women's creativity and power, it is not seen by most of the women we interviewed as the only space in which they shape their lives. It is true that the women we interviewed did emphasize the importance of staying home while their children were young. Many women who have not had children yet, such as Zdena, state that they would like to stay at home with their children 'as long as possible'. Women usually explained their desire to stay at home simply in terms of it being 'important' for a child to be with his/her mother. Some, such as Jana, offered a richer explanation: 'I'd like to stay at home with them as long as possible, so I don't miss out on the time they are growing up and I can give them the most of myself.' Reluctance to place very young children in day care, or to otherwise leave them in the hands of 'strangers', was also cited as a reason to take advantage of the current four-year maternity leave.

Furthermore, in describing what it means to be a 'good mother', women often focus on the amount of time a mother spends with her child. As Kamila put it, being a good mother is 'to know how to make time for the child'. A good mother is often defined in terms of the 'sacrifice' or 'devotion' a woman gives to her child. Finally, in describing the mother–child bond, most women define this relationship as extremely important and intense. It was most often expressed in terms of friendship, having someone to confide in, or knowing that there is someone you can always rely on. Kamila goes on to describe how she hopes she can 'raise the child so that they can tell me any problem they might have. . . . To be a good mother means to pay attention to your child and to know how to listen to him.' According to Magda, a good mother 'gives [her children] a foundation at home that they can lean on, so whatever happens, whenever, they can return to her and know they have a home'. For many women, the bond between mother and child does not end when the child reaches adulthood. As Renata puts it, 'this relationship should last all the way until the mother is eighty years old'.

It would be incorrect, however, to call these attitudes a return to 'traditional values', as so many Westerners seem tempted to do. For example, none of the women interviewed in this book describe their own mothers as full-time homemakers. The mothers of our informants were gainfully employed, sometimes as the single bread-winner in the family. This finding is hardly surprising, given the nearly universal female participation in the labour force under communism, the high divorce rate (approximately 20 per 100 mar-riages), and the legal practice of awarding custody largely to mothers (in 90 per cent of cases) (Heitlinger 1979, 1987).

In addition to mothers, our respondents' childhood experiences typically involved day care, being cared for by their grandmothers, or a combination of the two. In fact, it is precisely for this reason that many of them explain why they want to stay home. Helena, who spent much of her childhood on the sidelines of a racetrack where her mother and father worked, inherited her parents' pas-sion for horses, but decided to stay at home when her son was born. She says of her mother's career: 'It's not a job for a girl. It's very physically demanding and it is to the detriment of her family.'

GRANDMOTHERS

A number of women stressed the important role grandmothers played in raising them. 'The person I remember most from my childhood is my grandmother,' says Olina, 'She picked me and my sister up from school and spent a lot of time with us. Whatever my mother couldn't manage, grandma did.' Veronika also remembers her grand-mother as the one who filled in for her parents: 'My parents lived with my grandparents until I was fifteen, so when I was sick, grandma and grandpa – who were retired – took care of us, and my mother could normally go to work.' Describing how she imagines her own children will be raised, Magda laments, 'I won't have one of those grandmothers who'll take care of my children if I have them now because both my mother and step-mother have young children of their own. . . . I have to wait until they want grandchildren and have time for them. I think a grandmother is very important to a child. That's the person who spoils them.'

Magda isn't the only one who has to make do without her mother's help. The post-Revolution years have undermined the institution of 'grannies' in the Czech Republic. The sociological literature on grandmothers and great-grandmothers is not yet available, but it is a subject often covered in the popular press. According to an article in the *Prague Post*, which quotes the Research Institute of Labour and Social Affairs, the number of extended families living together has decreased by 50 per cent over the last twenty years. The demise of the extended family has gone hand-in-hand with the decline of the care-giving roles of grandmothers. Additionally, while the cost of living has skyrocketed, pensions have not kept up with inflation. This results in an overall decrease in pensioners' economic contributions to the family, and might lead to an overall decrease in grandmothers' and grandfathers' familial roles.

During the communist period, the extension of the maternal role to grandmothers was studied 'largely in connection with the problem of day-care centres and their impact on children. Another approach [was] to study grandmothers from the perspective of kinship, as a type of kin network of mutual assistance, not a type of extended family.' Social involvement of grannies in child rearing was generally higher among middle-class professional families than among single-parent or lower-class families, because the rules which governed admission to day nurseries favoured single and/or less educated mothers. This situation was often fraught with tensions, since women with a professional education were more likely to disagree with their mothers' (or mothers-in-law') views on children's upbringing than women who were less educated (Heitlinger, 1979, pp. 175–6).

Demographic statistics indicate that the average age at which Czech women became grandmothers was forty-five. With the retirement age being gradually extended from fifty-seven to sixty, and with women no longer employed in undemanding jobs, grandmothers are bound to find it more difficult to offer substantial child care assistance to their sons and daughters. As the role of grandmothers as caretakers wears away, mothers themselves are stepping in to fill the gap.

SHARING CHILD CARE BETWEEN MOTHERS AND FATHERS

All the women we spoke to initially stated that a child should be cared for by his/her mother. But further questioning revealed that their desire to see their children cared for is not necessarily based on strict gender roles that regard mothers as the sole care-takers.

When asked how they would feel about going to work and leaving their husbands at home with the children, the majority of women welcomed this idea. The main barrier to such arrangements tends to be money. When the question was posed in such a way that money was not an issue (i.e. women were asked to imagine they earn as much, or even more money than their husbands), most women answered that they would be happy to see their husbands as homemakers.

Some women even stated that it is 'natural' for the child to stay with his/her mother, but that economics could influence them to change this arrangement. This was most clearly expressed in Katka's answer: 'My husband would make a good mother. But I think it's decided by nature that the mother belongs with the children. She is the one who should be with them. But if you look at it from the economic standpoint, if her husband is earning a lot of money, she should stay with the baby as long as she is breastfeeding. But if she is earning more than him, he should stay at home.' Most women qualified their answers to explain that it is best for an infant to be with his/her mother, but for older children, the care of a father is just as good. As Zdena put it, 'if the child was just a baby, then no. But maybe after a year it would be OK. If my husband wanted it then I'd happily change places with him. The child would develop a relationship to his father. . . . Some men could take better care of them than some women. They can cook and clean.'

None of the women we interviewed are actually acting out these arrangements, though it is currently possible for fathers to take parental leave. That such flexible child care arrangements do, in fact, occur (though they are unusual) is evidenced by the arrangements in Magda's parents' household. 'When I was young my step-father was at home because his time is completely his own. He is a painter, so he is always at home,' Magda explains. 'Now he takes care of my step-sister. He takes her to school and picks her up and takes care of her through the day.'

While stressing the importance of staying at home with their child, women also told us that they were often frustrated by the day-to-day realities of being a housewife. The three or four years they had for maternity leave were described by many as boring or frustrating. Even though her maternity leave could have been extended another year, Veronika got fed up with being at home and went back to work after three years. Helena is looking for part-time work during which she will put her child in day care for a few hours a day. Olina is similarly attempting to find a way to return to work early because she feels cut off from any intellectual stimulation at home. As she puts it, 'originally I thought I would stay at home for three or more years. Now I think differently. . . . I feel that I've stopped growing. Or that I'm regressing. That I'm closed in. My thoughts go around in circles. I really miss hearing other people's opinions on things. . . . For that reason I'd go back to work, no matter what.' Significantly, women who had not yet had children stated that they would like to stay at home for much longer periods (6–7 years) than those who actually had children were willing to do (2–4 years).

AGE AT MARRIAGE AND MOTHERHOOD

Over half of the total number of women we interviewed were married before the age of twenty-four. Two out of the twenty-three were divorced. With one or two exceptions, all of the married women had children. Married and unmarried women alike agreed that a good age to have children was around twenty-five, and certainly before thirty. Thirty is therefore considered by many women as 'too old to have children'. This was not explained simply in terms of biology, but in terms of women's health and social relationships.

These views reflect the prevalent Czech medical advice that it is best to get pregnant while 20–25 years old. For example, Trča (1980, p. 25) argues in his popular advice book for women, *The Art of Healthy Living*, that 'during that period woman's fertility and health status are at their best, and in addition, the woman is mentally sufficiently mature to correctly raise her child'.

Many women thus regard over thirty as 'very old'. This attitude is exemplified in the words of Helena: 'Everywhere abroad they say to start [having kids] at thirty. But then when the child is ten, the mother is forty. I can't imagine her going ice-skating with the child. Or going swimming or skiing. Or playing with him. She'd be the kind of mother who would say, "go play with your friends". I try to have a more comradely relationship with my son. To be friends [with him].' Combining social and health factors, Katka similarly reasons: 'If [a woman] has [a child] at thirty-two, then even from a medical point of view, I don't think it is a good thing. And then can you imagine when the child is ten and she is forty-two? She could get cancer and never get to raise him! For all these reasons

I think around twenty is the best age.' Thus our study indicates that social factors, in particular women's conceptions of age, figure as prominently in pregnancy decisions as the medical considerations.

Even women such as Monika and Jana, who defended postponing motherhood, were aware of the medical arguments. As Monika explains, 'the medical experts say that presently in the Czech Republic, it's best for a woman to have children early because of the environmental problems here. Having children early lowers the risk of illness or miscarriage. But from my perspective, as a young woman, I think twenty-eight is the best age. But I told myself I would wait until I feel some maternal instinct within myself, until I feel like I really want a child, I need a child.' It is worth noting that 'although a strong relationship between environmental pollution and human health is widely assumed by health officials and the public [in Czechoslovakia], evidence for such a relationship is very limited at present, partly because the right kinds of study have not been conducted' (Bobak and Feachem, 1992, p. 240).

In explaining why it is important to have children young, a number of women also commented that it is important to be relaxed around a young child. If they were older, than they'd be 'too mature' and worry about the child breaking things or getting hurt. Katka explains, 'I think that at thirty, one is too anxious. I see how visitors react to Johnny when he climbs on something – "watch out!" they cry. I take things quite differently. I know nothing will happen to him. If he falls down, then he knows not to do it next time.'

And yet, despite this feeling that children are best cared for by the young, many women acknowledged that they themselves were cared for by their grandmothers. As previously mentioned, grandmothers used to play a significant role in raising children during the communist period. Perhaps this emphasis on youth is part of a larger devaluation of the elderly, although more research on this topic is required.

While there might be considerable rethinking of how, and by whom, a child should be raised, most women agree that it is essential for women to have children. As Renata puts it: 'Within all women there is something maternal that makes it so that she must have children.' Speaking more personally, Magda offers a very pragmatic reason for having children: 'Say I find a husband who is ten years older than me, then I'll be sixty and he will be seventy, and he'll die and I'll be left alone without any kids and without my parents.' Only Lenka stated that it is not necessary for every woman to have a child, although she emphasized that she herself would like to become a mother.

BEING A 'GOOD' MOTHER AND A 'GOOD' FATHER

While women value their roles as mothers quite highly, they nonetheless express ambiguity about what it means to be a good mother. Quite a few women, whether or not they have children, said that they did not know what it means to be a good mother, or that it is a difficult thing to achieve. Only two women drew upon examples of other women they knew, in both cases their own mothers.

There is even more ambivalence about fatherhood. Many women at first said that a good father is the same as a good mother, but when they continued on this theme, they described the roles of mother and father quite differently. According to our respondents, the most common characteristics of a 'good father' are: someone who provides financially for the family; is the source of authority; and spends time with his children. Unlike their descriptions of good mothers, the definition of a good father is often put in negative terms.

Women say that they don't want their husbands to be distant fathers (as so many of theirs were). A good father is 'not sitting in a bar all evening' says Zdena. Similarly, Olina describes a good father as spending as much time as possible with his children 'so the child knows he has a father and doesn't mistake him for an uncle'. Regardless of how much time their own fathers spent with them, many women described fathers in general as absent from the lives of children. As Magda put it, 'there's plenty of cases where the father has no idea what the children are up to. Then suddenly he finds out his child is drinking or smoking pot or his daughter is pregnant at sixteen. "How can this be!" he says. "She had everything." She had everything but was afraid to go to her mother or father because they would berate her or wouldn't have time for her.' Strikingly, while it is often unnecessary for mothers to be defined as liking or loving their children, this is not the case for fathers.

Many women also express ambivalence about motherhood, pointing out that along with its joys come many frustrations. 'The best part [of being a mother] is when the child smiles at you,' states Veronika. 'The worst is that you can't do what you want anymore. You have to take your child into account in everything.' A little more strongly put, Katka complains that 'the worst is getting up at night, I could shoot him.' Olina describes motherhood with the words: 'I spend my day with someone who needs me all the time. He's not interested in whether I have a headache of didn't get enough sleep. He just thinks, "I'm here now and I need my diaper changed!" But that's what's nice about it.' She goes on to say that she should have waited a few more years before having her son.

This ambivalence often extends to their relationships with their own mothers. Despite the strongly felt bond, many women expressed a need to break away from their parental homes, particularly from their mothers. The most extreme example is Milena, who states that due to her mother's emotional instability, her goal as a teenager was to move out. And the very fact that she managed to do so at the age of nineteen is quite remarkable. At twenty-four, Veronika would also like to move out and describes how difficult it is to raise her son while living with her parents. 'It's more like I'm helping my mom out, instead of her helping me out. It's her household, so she runs everything. . . . [When I lived on my own] I was not used to dealing with my mother's worries, which I have to do now.'

In fact, mothers do not figure prominently in most of the narratives. The reader does not get the impression that mothers influenced the nursing graduates' choice of partners, or that they dramatically affected their career plans. Yet, while women did not necessarily speak of them in these terms, many of their career choices did, in fact, follow in their mother's footsteps, be it in nursing or in some other field. The two best examples are Monika, who works for the media as does her mother, and Kamila, who has followed both her parents into policing. In some cases, this also reflects the importance of personal ties in job opportunities, which in the Czech Republic are still often being parcelled out along lines of interpersonal relationship. As under communism, connections to certain careers seem to make it easier for someone to gain a foothold in them (Mateju, 1992).

HOUSEWORK

Only one woman – Katka – claimed to enjoy the life of a classic 'housewife', and saw it as liberating. Katka enjoys being at home because, as she says, 'I can set my own schedule. . . . In the hospital

I had to listen to someone else. I don't like listening to someone else.' Most women expressed much more ambivalence. In fact, when asked if they would like to 'be a housewife', most women interpreted this to mean would they like to stay at home all the time, above and beyond the years they spend at home with young children while on maternity leave. The answer was always no.

In terms of who should do the housework, the majority of women expressed the view that it is desirable for men to help out, but that ultimately housework is a woman's job. For example, Lenka stated: 'It's good if the husband helps out. . . . But if he refused to do it – I think it's a woman's job.' Similarly, Veronika explains: 'The husband and wife should agree who should do it, but the primary work is the woman's.'

Sometimes, however, there was a distinct gap between how they thought housework should be parcelled out, and how it actually was divided. This comes through most clearly when Lenka describes what is 'men's work' as opposed to 'women's work':

> Men's work is to make sure the family is financially cared for. He makes sure that the broken washing machine gets fixed. Or he drives the car to the garage when it needs servicing. Otherwise the work around the house is women's work. Though you really can't say what is women's work. There's also the issue of who likes what, and what they can do. I just said a man should take the car to be serviced, but in our family I do the driving. My husband has a driver's license, but he almost never drives. He doesn't like it and it frightens him. So it's true that he cooks and I take the car to be fixed. With us it's the opposite of how it should be!

This difference between how things should be and how they are, is also expressed, from a different perspective, by Katka. When asked who should be responsible for the housework, she replies: 'Let me tell you first how we do it, then I'll tell you my opinion. With us, I of course take care of the household. That's because I am at home. But I think my husband could occasionally dry the dishes and vacuum, which he doesn't do.'

Lenka's, Veronika's and Katka's statements all reflect the common view that despite the differences between 'men's work' and 'women's work', housework is in fact something to be divided up by the two people involved. In making this claim, many women expressed their desire to divide the work in their household differently from how it was done in their parents' households. '[Housework should be done by] both people. Absolutely,' states Olina, 'It was different in my parents' household, but I'd like it this way.'

These changes in housework arrangements are often portrayed not only as changes between themselves and their parents, but as larger intergenerational changes. For example, as Magda comments, 'the wife used to have to go to work and take care of the home. Her husband would come home from work, pick up the paper and grab a beer, and sit in front of the TV. It definitely should not be like that.' Similarly, Zdena points out: 'Some older people are rooted in the idea that this is men's work and this is women's work and they won't touch the other person's jobs. I think that's stupid.' In rare cases, even their parent's households are seeing changes. Similarly to Magda's father, whose painting allows him to take care of his daughters at home, Katka's father has taken over many of the domestic activities. In his case, the reasons were financial. Since he's been unemployed, he's stayed at home and 'now he's the housewife'.

The definition of housework employed by Czech women differed from the Western use of the word. We first imagined 'housework' to mean jobs which in the West are associated with the classic housewife – doing dishes, laundry, cooking, etc. But Czech women define 'housework' as any domestic work, including jobs they categorized as 'men's work', such as fixing the laundry machine or cutting wood. This more comprehensive and encompassing definition reveals a sense of the house/home as a more inclusive domain, that requires the labour of both men and women to maintain it. Re-defining 'housework' more broadly as 'domestic work' requiring the complementary labour of both spouses tends to undermine the popular image of the 'home' as the private (and exclusive) domain of women.

PAID WORK

Work outside the home is described as an important realm in women's lives. The majority of women express agency in determining their work choices. This is clearly manifested by the fact that only four out of the fourteen women interviewed for this book are currently working as nurses. Three others are at home on maternity leave, while the remaining seven have left nursing for other, more lucrative jobs. Most of the women in our study have demonstrated their commitment to paid work and occupational advancement by moving 'up' from one field to another. They studied foreign languages, such as English and German, learned computer skills, or even went back to school. Renata left nursing to work as a teacher and hopes soon to receive her certificate in special education. Lenka is a co-manager of a property business. Jana went back to school to study psychology.

Even those who stayed in nursing express this as a choice, and consider their work important. For example, Olina (who is currently on maternity leave) never wanted to be a nurse, but once enrolled in a nursing school, she found her training interesting. Upon completion, she decided to work in the most challenging ward – the emergency room. In describing her work there she says: 'I liked the responsibility. The trust that everybody had in me. Doctors couldn't be with their patients all the time, but I could. So they had to believe what I told them.'

Social contacts established at the workplace, typically expressed as 'being in a collective', were seen as another positive benefit of working. This was stressed by our respondents, both for themselves and for their mothers. At the same time, however, most of the women in our study were highly critical of the boredom of clerical jobs, and of the misuse of power at work. Veronika complains of the tedium of being a secretary, describing her work as 'basically administrative work. Pick up the phone, make the coffee, type something up. Nothing special. And when there's nothing to do, then it's especially boring.'

Jana complains that when she was a nurse 'none of the doctors spent time with us, told us what they were doing, and why'. Instead, as numerous women comment, doctors treat nurses like maids, expecting them to clean up. 'Maybe I'm a little bit vain,' Jana continues, 'but it bothered me when the doctors treated us like cleaners. We had a lot of work but we did janitorial work because there were no cleaners. It bothered me not to get any respect, not to have my work given any regard. Because the work should be respected.' Petra had similar complaints about the lack of recognition of the work nurses perform. In her view, it is not just doctors but society as a whole who are to blame: 'Everybody still assumes nursing is not hard work and that we sleep with doctors. I don't think people realize how difficult it is to be a nurse.'

COMBINING DOMESTIC IDENTITIES WITH WORK IDENTITIES

While highlighting the importance of their role in the domestic sphere, most of the women expressed a desire to combine both worlds of work and home-life. As Helena puts it: 'Women are born in order to have children. Not to have careers. I think you can manage both, but I don't appreciate women who never have children.' Later she goes on to explain why she thinks that women are better off in life than men: 'A girl has a much more varied life. She has a child, then goes back to work. Then maybe she has another child.'

As Czech sociologist Jiřina Šiklová (1993, p. 76) points out, Czech women have a complex relationship to the meaning of work in their lives:

> Despite the fact that 76 percent of women polled in 1991 stated that they worked primarily to better provide for their families, 40 percent also said that they would not leave their jobs even if their husband had a sufficiently high income. These answers suggests a certain discrepancy in logic, which reflects women's ambivalent stand on employment, politics, and their own identities.

Based on our findings, part of the confusion is that most Czech women are not totally fulfilled by either their careers or by the role of mother/housewife. Instead, they strive towards a more complex combination of both roles. Just as it is incorrect to regard them as retreating into the domestic space of the housewife, it is incorrect to place their views of work within the Western feminist paradigm of paid work as a form of liberation. While work does form a large part of their identities, most women do not assert themselves through their work situations *per se*, nor through their domestic arrangements, but through a synthesis of the two.

REACTIONS TO FEMINISM

The sentiments described above may help to explain much of the Czech women's negative reaction to Western feminism. As Heitlinger (1996, p. 90) has argued, Western feminism does not strike a deep responsive chord with Czech women (and men) because most Czechs mistrust utopian and emancipatory ideologies; associate concepts such as 'women's emancipation', 'women's equality' and 'women's movement' with the policies of the discredited paternalistic communist regime; are disinclined to engage in collective action; regard themselves as strong women rather than as victims; assign highly positive meaning to motherhood and the family, and perceive feminism to be anti-male. The world view of Czech women is informed by the social legacy of communism, and as such it currently lies outside the descriptive and theoretical frameworks of Anglo-American feminism.

In our study, Magda did not like the tendency of Western feminism to put special emphasis on women's roles outside of the home. In an interesting, though very confusing twist, Monika describes feminists as resolutely against abortion. Her comments reflect the distorted notions Czech women (and men) tend to have of 'Western feminism'. 'While women affiliated with the Gender Studies Center in Prague have been able to learn about Western feminism directly from feminist literature, from Western feminists who now live in Prague, and/or from those who have visited the Czech capital,' Heitlinger (1996, pp. 86–7) argues, 'the vast majority of Czech women have never met a Western feminist, and have never read any of the literature. Their ideas of Western feminism are based on two decades of misrepresentation by the communist press without any exposure to the other side, the derogatory portrayal of Western feminists by the postcommunist media, and their own pre-conceived ideas about Western affluence. The negative reaction to feminism is of course also strengthened by the real experiences Czech women have had with official Marxist feminism under communism.'

Only two women in our study said something positive about feminism. Milena makes a passing remark about women struggling for emancipation, and Kamila strongly defends women against sexist stereotypes. Kamila goes on to claim that communist rule promoted women's rights. And in her discussion of the influential book on feminism that she read, Kamila is unique in showing an interest in learning about Western feminist thought.

PUBLIC SPACE, POLITICS AND RELIGION

Beyond the world of work, public space is not seen as a place of power or self-realization. Only one woman, Zdena, mentions politics as important to her. Yet while expressing a desire to have her opinions represented in political decisions, she is not hopeful that she will be able to realize this. Thus she is not active in politics, and doesn't even plan to vote until she is older. Zdena also expresses the common sentiment against involvement in organizations of any kind. When asked if she belongs to any professional associations, she answers, 'No. No associations. I think they are worthless. I'm sick of how we always had to be members of some kind of organization. Take the Red Cross. I joined it the minute I started nursing school. . . . Nothing ever came out of it. So I'm not interested. I don't want to be in any groups, any associations, anything like that.'

Our interviews suggest that this reluctance extends to organized religion. As we noted in Chapter 2, Czech opinion polls estimate that four out of five Czechs define themselves as either atheist or agnostic. While six out of the fourteen women included in this book state that they have some religious beliefs, these tend to be highly individualistic or connected to their families, not to a religious community as a whole. For example, Monika describes her religious sentiments in terms of lying alone in bed, terrified of death. Renata speaks of going to church as a young child as something she did with her grandmother. Jana (off tape) discusses Christianity as something important to her family as a whole. Not one of the six 'believers' describes the religious community as having any influence on their religious beliefs. Reflecting the widespread secularism of the Czech population, the majority of our respondents define themselves as non-believers and as not belonging to any kind of organized religious groups.

INDIVIDUALISM

Many of the sentiments described above can best be understood as part of a rhetoric of intense individualism. It is impossible to overstate how often and in how many diverse contexts this sentiment is expressed. The concept of individualism often came up when women mentioned the various opportunities they now have in their lives. For example, Milena said of her life after the revolution: 'It's up to me what my limits are.' When asked who is better off in life, men or women, Magda responds: 'That's completely individual. It's completely up to me how I am and completely up to the guy how he is.'

In a more complicated view of individualism, Alexandra critiques the way that many people are unable to relate to her husband as a complete human being now that he is in a wheelchair. While she and her husband have developed friendships with other disabled people, Alexandra does not suggest that they should combat these misperceptions together. Instead she states: 'I think that what a person doesn't fight for, they don't get. I think there are plenty of organizations here to help out, but basically it's up to the individuals.'

References to individualism also came up with respect to the issue of abortion. Most women view abortion as a choice. Even those who oppose abortion on moral grounds do not think it should be illegal. In fact, out of the twenty-three women interviewed, including three who describe themselves as 'very religious', not one states that there should be severe restrictions on access to abortion. Instead, many of them stress that women have reasons for having abortions and should be allowed to have them, even if they know that what they are doing is 'wrong'. As Veronika expresses it, 'I don't like it but I wouldn't make it illegal. If a woman submits herself to it, then she knows why.'

SEXUALITY

While the interview questions did not ask anything specific about sexuality, the topic did come up in a few of the interviews. Similarly to the discussion of abortion, our respondents stress the necessity of women having greater control over reproduction. Their views reflect the greater openness on issues of sexuality since the Velvet Revolution, which has also been documented in other studies. For example, Lisa Mulholland (1993) details the rise in pornography (aimed at both male and female consumers), along with the prominent displays of affection by couples in the Prague metro, as new signs of more open and more public sexuality since the revolution. In her analysis of lesbian activism in Prague, Susanna Trnka (1993) shows that while lesbian organizations may still have a number of barriers to overcome, lesbian visibility has grown rapidly since the revolution.

Speaking from a personal perspective, Petra points out the greater openness in society since 1989 when she states:

When I was fifteen there was no problem in going to the doctor for contraceptives. But who at that age would go to a gynecologist? We had no sexual education in elementary school nor in high school. . . . It's completely different if the subject is treated openly and discussed with the child from a young age, both at home, with parents, and at school. After the Revolution, magazines for young people started coming out. It was discussed at school.

FAMILIAL INDIVIDUALISM

Since so many women see themselves as embedded within the family, the question arises whether it is at all possible to talk about individualism in this context. What we would like to propose is that many Czech women believe in, and act on, a particular conception of 'familial individualism'. They see society as structured around the individual, as opposed to larger community groups, and at the same time, view their individual choices as shaped by their families. Thus they try to balance their sense of freedom as individuals with their role as members of a family. One example is Lenka's response to whether or not she would like to go to college. She answers, 'Maybe I'd go to school except that I've already been married for two and half years and we're planning a family. . . . If I was single I'd go to college. But since I'm married, I don't think I'd enjoy student life.'

Similarly, Veronika wants to go back to being a nurse but can't do that while taking care of her son, so she chooses 'boring' work close to home as a secretary. In a more complicated example, Magda explains she doesn't like feminism because it promotes equal pay for men and women. 'It is logical that a man should be paid more than a woman when it is he who supports the family,' she says. When asked: 'What about if a woman is on her own?', she responds: 'Then that's another thing. You have to ask why she's on her own. I'm talking on the assumption that it's a normally functioning family. A woman alone – that's bad. But then why is she on her own? I think that a person is always able to find some kind of partner who will suit them. If he's not able to do that, then that's his short-coming.' Clearly, Magda has trouble imagining a woman living outside of a family (despite her statements earlier on in the interview when she stated that she would not mind being a single mother).

This sense of being embedded in a family also comes through in terms of the kinds of questions women seem to be asking themselves, such as: how many kids can we afford to raise? must I go to work or can my husband support me to stay at home? maybe I would like to go to work just for myself? what is best for my child? Thus when women speak of 'individualism', they may not be using the term in personal sense but rather in a familial sense.

In contrast to the communist period, women today see their roles and their opportunities in society as individual choices rather than as socially proscribed norms. It's up to them how they divide the housework, or whether or not they have an abortion. Things don't have to be the way their parents did it, or even according to the way 'nature' makes it. And yet, at the same time, they see their freedom as individuals as clearly restricted within the bounds of their family.

LIFE STRATEGIES

One of the primary foci of this study was young women's 'life strategies', the types of goals they set up for themselves, and how they plan to attain them. At first glance, many of the women expressed a rather strong sense of goalessness. They often spoke about drifting aimlessly through life. Renata says of her adolescence. 'I don't remember having any dreams of who I could be. I just accepted what came.' Jana describes similar feelings of aimlessness as a teenager; 'It didn't even occur to me that I could do something different or that I could go somewhere to study or go away for a longer period of time. I was raised to think that I would finish school and get a job.'

Many women extend this feeling of aimlessness past adolescence and into their present lives. As Alexandra puts it, 'I am not the kind of person to plan far ahead. I wanted to finish school and get a job, that's all. What will come will come. I never had any future plans.' At the same time, it is pretty clear that their lives are not completely uncharted. They do express agency in shaping their personal and workplace lives. As stated earlier, they make and act on career goals by pursuing more training, studying foreign languages, learning computer skills, or even starting their own businesses. They also set personal goals such as moving out of their parents' homes, starting a family or having more children.

One possible reason why they express such aimlessness might be due to an initial reluctance to state their goals to the interviewer. In two cases, the more time the interviewer spent with the participant, the more concrete future plans they expressed. Jana, for example, was interviewed twice. In the first interview, she said she had no plans for her future. But by the second interview, she was outlining a clear plan to travel, learn a foreign language, finish college and perhaps return to nursing.

Similarly, when Alexandra was first asked what her future plans were, she said that she had none. However, once the tape recorder was turned off, she told the interviewer that she and her husband are in fact thinking of starting some kind of business, though she did not divulge any of the details. At the end of what turned out to be a lengthy three-hour interview, Alexandra revealed that if her husband remains in a wheelchair, they would like to open a car repair shop based in their backyard. It is therefore possible that other participants, though very aware of their future plans, were reticent in stating their goals to the interviewer, and so kept silent about them.

Part of their reluctance may have been out of modesty. We were told by several American business advisors working in Prague that Czech job applicants are not as bold as their American counterparts. In situations such as job interviews, where an American would be more likely to embellish upon their job qualifications, a Czech is more likely, out of modesty, to diminish them. Another factor may be a Czech cultural norm suggesting that it is inadvisable to speak of something that has not yet happened. For example, we have encountered over the years numerous Czech immigrants in Canada and the US who found the North American practice of having a 'baby shower' before the baby is born rather peculiar, since such celebration might bring 'bad luck' to the birth. Since North American culture is a culture of 'optimism', notions of negative outcomes tend not to figure prominently in the beliefs and actions of many Canadians and Americans.

In Alexandra's case there was the added problem of not knowing whether her husband would walk again. Since her main desire was to see him get better, this made the formulation of a 'backup' plan, which would accept his disability as permanent, doubly difficult.

FAMILY CONTROL

In a few of the interviews, participants spoke of being forced by their families to accept limitations on their opportunities of life. Veronika describes how she wanted to be a doctor, but her husband did not want her to go to college. 'He didn't want me to do it and at that time I was in love with him so I didn't. I started working as a nurse and there was peace between us,' she explains. Later on in the interview she implies that part of her husband's control over her was economic. Kamila's limitations came from her husband after they were divorced. She was forced to leave her job when her husband continually showed up drunk at her place of work. Jana tells how her mother was one exam away from qualifying as a teacher when her father stopped her: 'She had to commute to her classes, so he brought her home and guarded her. He didn't let her go anywhere. So she didn't finish.'

While it is impossible to estimate how prevalent this phenomenon is, domestic violence was brought up a number of times in the interviews. More often than not, it was discussed after the tape recorder was turned off. For example, one of the women interviewed but not included in this collection, painfully recalled (off tape) that her father used to violently discipline her for the smallest infraction, and that his behaviour has had profoundly negative consequences on her ability to assert herself in life. In a less personal way, violent behaviour towards children is discussed by Renata, who works in a school for abused children. Another participant (not included here) spoke of her work as a therapist for adults who were sexually abused as children. Finally, though it is only by implication, Jana alludes to the frequency of such behaviour in her comment that 'surely you can raise [your children] without hitting them every night.'

THE VELVET REVOLUTION

The number of women who state that the revolution had no effect on their lives was startling to us. Many echo Veronika's statement that 'for me there was no revolution. My life is the same. I can't say it was better before, but it hasn't changed.' Most women mention that they were too young to realize the impact of the previous regime on their lives. They also think of 1989 as a time of their own personal development, as the shift from youth to young adulthood, when they began establishing their own family and work lives. In general, they emphasize that the personal life-cycle changes were more important to them then than the larger social–political–economic upheavals going on around them.

In some cases this was due to extreme circumstances, such as Kamila's, whose father passed away during the revolution. But even the less extreme personal experiences of graduating and finding job often took precedence in their narratives. As Milena explains, 'my plans changed but that was because I grew up, not because there was a revolution'. Many women implied that by 1989 they felt that their lives were already following a set course and that the revolution came too late to have an impact on them. In pre- and post-interview chats, women often brought up the issue of education and how students in school after 1989 have had the opportunity of learning English or German, something they themselves missed out on. They furthermore implied that it is not for them, but for today's teenagers and children that the situation has changed the most. This sense of having reached adulthood, and of their lives as being somehow 'established' by the age of eighteen, relates to their rather rigid conceptions of age and adulthood (as discussed earlier).

It is interesting to compare the way women spoke of the period of the revolution and how they described the four years they spent in nursing school. If there was a time of generalized change and upheaval in their lives, it was when they entered nursing school at fourteen rather than the revolution of 1989. In fact, many women speak of nursing school as a time of 'moral crisis', when they first had to face death and dying. As Jana puts it,

at the age of fourteen, I went a number of times to watch dissections. I saw dead bodies opened up. At fourteen it really changed me. At that age you are still almost a child and suddenly you see horrible wounds. In nursing school, when I was fifteen, sixteen, seventeen, I met people who were dying. At such an age, as long as one of your relatives doesn't die, you don't even think about such things. It was very difficult.

Petra went through a similar experience but not until she was already working as a nurse:

When I was eighteen and started working in intensive care, I was shocked by how many young people were dying there. This I was not prepared for. Our practice sessions were in the internal medicine ward, where we saw old grandmothers. But when you cannot help young people. . . . It was too soon to see that. It changed me. It took a long time to get used to.

Despite the fact that many of the strikers during the 1989 Revolution were students, none of the women we interviewed were active in the revolution. Instead, they seem to regard the revolution as something that occurred outside of them, and that may or may not have a positive impact upon their lives. One woman – Helena – explains why she was, in fact, opposed to joining the strikers: 'When the other girls came and told me they were at a strike rally on Wenceslas Square that day, I thought "What were they doing there? They would only get beaten up." I am very conservative in these things. I didn't really experience the revolution. I accepted that things changed, but I didn't really care.'

Other women were quite clear that the revolution had profound consequences on their lives. Jana, for example, states: 'There are a lot more opportunities to develop myself and generally learn things. . . . I am discovering life, new people, and how people live elsewhere.' Regardless of how our respondents themselves assessed the impact of the revolution on their lives, the evidence presented in the interviews suggests a profound impact in a number of areas. For example, women now have new fields of employment to choose from. Under communism, Lenka could have never become a co-manager of a real estate agency. Women now also have more opportunities to learn a foreign language other than Russian. They can also return to school and study new disciplines which were unavailable under the previous regime. But the greatest impact upon their lives appears to be the increasing importance of money.

MONEY

The majority of women expressed an awareness of a new society powered by money. Money was seen as the defining factor in life chances, and the nursing graduates often saw themselves as disadvantaged in this respect. Monika explains: 'Money guarantees freedom. It's a means of being really free. It's fantastic if someone travels to Bali and meditates, but you need to have money to get to Bali. You need to have the means to realize your freedom.' Monika has enough money to travel, but many other women looked at it from a different perspective. Thus, Katka complains: 'What is it worth to me that the borders are open and I could go to America if I don't have the money?'

Money has also become a major factor in making life decisions. For Olina it determines whether or not she and her husband can afford to have more children. For Veronika it means she has to work as a secretary instead of as a nurse. Even though situations such as these may seem self-evident to the Western reader familiar with the workings of a market economy, for a large number of Czechs using money as a basis on which to construct people's identities and 'worth' is something new.

Thus even those respondents who did not hold money in high regard recognized its social importance. Zdena, for example, declares that she likes the way her mother raised her, even though they didn't have much money: '[Our mom] didn't have a lot of money to shower us with presents. But we had a nice environment. . . . I'd try to do it the same way.' Magda similarly asserts: 'I definitely know that money and a high salary are not the most important things for me.' In both cases, their assertions are defences against both the growing social inequality and the prevalent rhetoric that money really is important.

Irrespective of whether or not respondents regarded money as personally important to them, many strongly criticized its current importance in society. 'Now we are ruled by money,' Zdena asserts. 'Those who have money have it all. In some ways, it's very cruel.' Olina claims: 'Society is harder now than before. Take for example my husband's business. It prospers or goes into debt. It's based on his abilities and what he's doing.' Finally, despite their criticisms, and the deep ambivalence they expressed about some of the political issues that the revolution has brought on (such as privatization), nobody stated that they want to go back to old regime.

FREEDOM AND CHOICE

The concept of 'freedom' was rarely raised. With the exception of Monika's equation of freedom with money, no one else offered a definition of freedom or even used the term. Instead, they often spoke of 'choice'. Many women asserted that the new democracy has enabled them to have more choices in their lives – choices that they often may not actually be able to realize.

With the exception of Katka, most women regard their ability to travel as very important for them, even though they may not actually have the money to do so. The importance of travel could be also interpreted in light of their focus on individualism. In citing the many benefits the revolution has brought them, very few women state increased access to information from the West (such as newspapers, books, or television). Instead, they stress travel – the opportunity to go and see for themselves what life is like beyond the former Iron Curtain.

Like travel, the ability to buy more and more varied products is expressed as another important change. Lenka's comparison of life in the East and the West is captured by her memory of walking through a West German supermarket as a young girl: 'You went to the store and there were twenty kinds of yoghurt. That didn't exist here at all. . . . We had just one kind of yoghurt – white, with marmalade at the bottom. It sounds quite petty, but as a child, that's what I noticed.' While Lenka laughs at how 'petty' this comparison is, Veronika asserts the importance of commodities in both her adolescent and her adult life. Explaining that the revolution really did not effect her, Veronika says: 'when I got older and wanted jeans, we had to go to Tuzex [foreign currency shop]. Now jeans are everywhere and I still can't afford them. Things have changed but not in a way that really reached me.'

Zdena takes it one step further when she states that the most important benefit of the revolution for her is that 'now the shops are full of goods. I can window shop from morning till evening and look at beautiful things.' Zdena speaks of looking, but she doesn't actually speak of buying anything. Instead, she relates window shopping to travelling, another important opportunity that she doesn't have the money to realize. Thus the very possibility of having so many choices of commodities is seen as important, regardless of whether or not they can actually be purchased. Finally, reminiscent of Slavenka Drakulic's (1992) defence of Yugoslav women's right to buy fur coats, Monika asserts the importance of newly available beauty products. Like Drakulic, Magda stresses women's rights to commodities that make them 'beautiful'.

IMPORTANCE OF BEAUTY

Monika not only comments on the importance of beauty products, but on the importance of cultivating beauty itself. 'When I see a pretty girl and a pretty guy, it lifts my spirits more than if I see someone ugly,' she explains. 'I want to go out into society and not look like some poor Cinderella. I'm not saying I make a star out of myself, but I care how I look.' 'But Czechs are only just learning how to cultivate beauty', she adds. 'Unlike in the West where for generations [women] have seen commercials and been told to buy creams for their faces, we didn't have that until six years ago.'

Monika, in fact, exaggerates the extent to which communist Czechoslovakia lacked fashion and make-up industries. Contrary to what Monika says, *Indulona* was not the only face cream product available on the socialist market. However, she is right in asserting that the choice of make-up products was limited. Apart from the special foreign currency Tuzex shops, it was indeed impossible before 1989 to buy any cosmetic products imported from the West. Jewellery and fashionable clothing were also available under communism, but consumer choice was again limited to domestic products.

It was also possible to buy expert personal advice books, written for women, young couples or three-generational households. The very title of one such book, *A Woman = Health + Beauty* (*Žena = Zdravie + Krása*), published in Slovakia in 1978, clearly emphasizes the importance of women's physical attractiveness (Bárdoš, 1978).

While Monika is the only woman to explicitly talk about the importance of beauty, many women revealed similar viewpoints through their appearances. Most, but not all, of the respondents came to the interview impeccably dressed, often wearing make-up and jewellery. It was not uncommon for them to have dyed their hair and to be wearing very fashionable outfits. While it is difficult to judge how they dress for everyday purposes, they obviously put a lot of care into their appearances. Many women, furthermore, commented that they were on diets, or that they went to the gym to improve their figures.

While the interviewer made every effort to match the care they put into their appearances, she did notice considerable difference in the way women reacted to her based on her appearance. On days when she wore her hair pulled back in a pony tail, and kept her glasses on, she received a fair share of negative looks. Some women even commented that she would look better if she let her hair down. She soon learned that having her hair down, wearing contacts instead of glasses, and a touch of lipstick, tended to make the interviews run smoother.

CONTACT WITH THE WEST

Another outcome of the revolution has been increased contact with the West. Various estimates suggest that anywhere from ten to forty thousand American expatriates live in Prague, along with large numbers of Western Europeans. McDonalds and Kentucky Fried Chicken restaurants now dot the city, and American and Western European TV shows have taken over the prime-time air waves. Most of these developments were heavily criticized by the women we interviewed. Katka, for example, complains that all of the shows on TV used to be Russian, and now they are all American. Magda is the most outspoken, asserting, before the interview even started, that she dislikes Americans, would never like to go to America, and doesn't like the way Americans and Germans have been driving the prices up in Prague.

Criticism of Americans and other Westerners was often expressed in terms of money and power relations. Many women pointed out that young American expatriates have more opportunities in Prague than they themselves have. Americans can afford to travel, go to restaurants and, in contrast to most Prague natives, rent apartments at prices well beyond what the average Czechs can afford.

Closer contacts, though similarly maligned, exist with Germany. Many women have worked, or hope to work, in Germany. Petra, for example, worked in a nursing home in Germany, Helena's husband currently works in Berlin, and one woman (not included in this collection) who married a German businessman now spends most of the year living in Germany. The interviewer was also told by several respondents that the reason why she could not contact some of their classmates was because they were currently working abroad.

While women did not use the language of 'exploitation' to describe their relationships with Americans or Germans, they did continually stress that they were not benefiting from the Westernization of the Czech Republic. They tended to view their position as the weaker partner in an unbalanced relationship. In fact, much of their unhappiness was expressed in terms of lack of opportunities they have in comparison to Westerners: they would like to have a bigger piece of what is actually 'their' pie.

RELATIONSHIP TO THE INTERVIEWER

In meeting with their Czech-American interviewer, most women considered this as an opportunity to ask questions about the United States. As described in the introductory chapter, they were primarily interested in questions such as whether life in the United States is really like it appears on American television shows, how is education structured in the US, and whether the availability of apartments is as much of a problem in US cities as it is in Prague. Many women asked the interviewer quite personal questions, often in the context of balancing motherhood and career. The most common question posed to the interviewer, who identified herself as being twenty-four years old, unmarried and without children, was when did she plan to have children. Many of the women implied that it was high time she did so, and were pleased to hear that she hopes to starts a family fairly soon. While they were very curious about her plans for child care, no one suggested that she gives up her academic position, just that she not overlook her 'natural' role as a woman.

CONCLUSION

Our findings indicate that the women in our study do in fact comprise a 'new generation' of young women in the Czech Republic. Born in the 1970s and coming of age the very year of the Revolution, they are – consciously and unconsciously – living out new life strategies that distinguish them from their predecessors. Not only are they undertaking new domestic arrangements, but they are also embarking upon more co-operative parenting strategies than did their parents before them. Most markedly, they are drawing their sense of self-esteem and recognition not only from their roles as mothers, nor from their roles in the working world, but from a complex combination of their identities as workers and mothers. They are not, however, investing the same meaning into their activities in public space (i.e. politics, social groups, religion).

The members of this new generation are actively interpreting the political, economic and social changes of the Velvet Revolution in terms of life strategies that often revolve around the issue of choice. But, as they are well aware, the choices available to them are often tempered by the Czech Republic's role as a 'lesser' power as compared, on a global economic scale, to the United States or Germany. Their ability to act upon these choices is also influenced by a rhetoric of intense individualism. This individualism is understood not on an 'individual' level, but on a familial level. It compels them to view their choices in terms of a negotiation between their personal goals and the needs of their families as a whole, and outside of wider, community or societal groups. Even in their awareness of the limitations put upon them – be it due to money, familial pressures, or education – the new generation stresses the importance of living in a world of choices, despite the fact that they might not actually be able currently to take advantage of these choices. Thus the increase in availability of commodities, the ability of travel, and the opportunity to learn foreign languages are hailed by them as some of the most important developments brought on by the revolution.

It will be interesting to see how, and if, the life-views of this new generation manifest themselves in their children. Will they too stress the importance of living in a world of choices, even if such choices are not realistically available to them? Or will their awareness of their economic, social and political vulnerability lead them to be even more critical of their lack of power? How will they balance their roles as individuals, family members, and potential members of larger community groups? Only time and future research can tell. But if the women in our study have their say, the next generation will have even more life opportunities than they do.

REFERENCES

Bárdoš , Augustín (1978), *Žena = Zdravie + Krása. Sprievodca modernej Žieny* (Osveta: Martin).
Bobak, Martin and Feachem, Richard G.A. (1992), 'Health Status in the Czech and Slovak Federal Republic', *Health Policy and Planning*, **7** (3), pp. 234–42.

Drakulic, Slavenka (1992), *How We Survived Communism and Even Laughed* (London: Hutchinson).

Heitlinger, Alena (1979), *Women and State Socialism: Sex Inequality in the Soviet Union and Czechoslovakia* (London: Macmillan).

Heitlinger, Alena (1987), *Reproduction, Medicine and the Socialist State* (London: Macmillan; New York: St Martin's Press).

Heitlinger, Alena (1993), 'The Impact of the Transition from Communism on the Status of Women in the Czech and Slovak Republics', in Nanette Funk and Magda Mueller (eds), *Gender Politics and Post-Communism. Reflections from Eastern Europe and the Former Soviet Union* (New York and London: Routledge), pp. 95–108.

Heitlinger, Alena (1995), 'Women's Equality, Work and Family in the Czech Republic', in Barbara Lobodzinska (ed.), *Family, Women, and Employment in Central-Eastern Europe* (Westport, CT: Greenwood Press), pp. 87–99.

Heitlinger, Alena (1996), 'Framing Feminism in Post-Communist Czech Republic', *Communist and Post-Communist Studies*, **29** (1), pp. 77–93.

McClune, Emma (1996), 'Changes in Czech Society are Pulling Apart the Traditional Extended Family', *The Prague Post*, 21–27 February.

Matějů, (1992), 'Beyond Educational Inequality in Czechoslovakia', *Czechoslovak Sociological Review*, **28**, pp. 37–60.

Matynia, Elzbieta (1995), 'Finding a Voice: Women in Postcommunist Central Europe', in Amrita Basu (ed.), *The Challenge of Local Feminisms: Women's Movements in Global Perspective* (Boulder, CO: Westview Press), pp. 374–404.

Mulholland, Lisa (1993), 'Kissing on the Subway: Sexuality and Gender in the Czech Republic', in Susanna Trnka (with Laura Busheikin) (ed.), *Bodies of Bread and Butter. Reconfiguring Women's Lives in the Post-Communist Czech Republic* (Prague: Gender Studies Centre), pp. 55–8.

Šiklová, Jiřina (1993), 'Are Women in Eastern Europe Conservative', in Nannette Funk and Magda Mueller (eds), *Gender, Politics and Post-Communism. Reflections from Eastern Europe and the Former Soviet Union* (New York and London: Routledge), pp. 74–83.

Trča, Stanislav (1980), *Umění zdravě žít. Kniha pro ženy* (Prague: Avicenum).

Trnka, Susanna (1993), 'First We Need a Room: Lesbian Activism in the Czech Republic', in Susanna Trnka (with Laura Busheikin) (ed.), *Bodies of Bread and Butter. Reconfiguring Women's Lives in the Post-Communist Czech Republic* (Prague: Gender Studies Centre), pp. 45–9.

Wolchik, Sharon (1992), 'Women's Issues in Czechoslovakia in the Communist and Post-Communist Periods', in B. Nelson and N. Chowdhury (eds), *Women and Politics Worldwide* (New Haven, CT: Yale University Press).